The Way of the Ways
Book One

Lao Tzŭ: TAO

The
Way of
The Ways

1.
Lao Tzŭ:
TAO

2.
The Prophetic
WORD

3.
John Woolman:
PURE WISDOM

4.
Gandhi:
TRUTH

The Way of the Ways

Book One

Lao Tzǔ: TAO

The Tao Teh Ching
Translation/Commentary

(Revised)

Herrymon Maurer

New Claypole Publishing, Inc.
Trumansburg, New York

For more information, please contact:

New Claypole Publishing, Inc.
http://www.newclaypole.org

Formatter's Note: This print version of the book was converted from the author's original Microsoft Word for MS-DOS files to QuarkXPress 2018 by Glenn Picher of Dirigo Multimedia, Inc. (http://www.dmulti.com). The author's original manual hyphenations and right-justified line endings have been preserved, as he took great care to format lines visually, sometimes even rewriting sentences for a more seamless flow for the reader. (The electronic version of this book, by contrast, has been reformatted to use flexible hyphenation and reflowable paragraphs and pages, to accommodate varying screen sizes on reader devices, and includes many hyperlinks for easier navigation.) Both editions incorporate minor updates in usage and time spans to reflect the 2018 date of publication, though the author died in 1998.

The Way of the Ways

Book One. Lao Tzŭ: TAO

IN MEMORIAM
HU SHIH
CHOU LI-FEI

Preface

The Way
of the Ways

It is said by one of the great prophetic teachers of the eighteenth century that "so long as a man looks only at himself he cannot but despair, but so long as he looks at the creation around him, he will know joy." The choice belongs to every man, woman, and child who comes into the world. Each one can relate the universe to himself or himself to the universe. In the first case, he can try to see all the sticks and stones of creation and all human thoughts and imaginations—all life itself—as they relate to him; he can make every effort literally to explain the universe, dominate it, and believe himself master of it. Or he can see himself as part of it, accepting its essential mysteriousness not as something deflating and threatening but as something exciting and life-giving.

For there are only two basic ways of being, living, thinking: a narrow way of logic and reason, the way of explanation; and the broader way that includes logic and reason but goes beyond them to embrace every aspect of the human personality—the unconscious as well as the conscious, the psychological as well as the concrete, the realms of the spirit as well as those of the material, the physical and the mental. This unity within the human being and its corresponding unity with the universe around it are the true source of meaningfulness: not the meaning of this, that, and the other, but their inherent but hidden purposiveness and wholeness.

The dichotomy is in no way between science and religion. In their own ways, both can be rigid, creedal, dogmatic, manipulative, narrowly logical, and sometimes incapable of fresh contact with factual reality. These tendencies, redolent of the thought of ancient Greece, have existed in the Western world for many centuries, and for many decades at least in more distant parts. The mind-set is central to the conventional Western way of being and thinking, whether liberal, conservative, radical, or authoritarian. The mind-set is inherent also in egocentrism, in willful pursuit of what enhances (in popular but vulgar parlance) "number one," in short, greed, ostentation, deceit, oppression, and ultimately violence.

It should be evident to human beings everywhere that these predilections have increased rather than allayed the miseries so rife among contemporary men and women both personally and socially. Inherent in them is a denial that human beings are social animals. When people think of themselves before they think of their relationship with others, they can become subject to self-seeking in the form of enhancement of self or in the form of denigrating of self. Low ego fixes attention on self no less powerfully and possibly even more miserably than high ego.

Separatism is the common attribute of conventional existence; people by the billions have been cut off from one another, not so much by the exigencies of geography as by the notion that individuals and groups can justify themselves and find emotional solace in sundering themselves from their fellows: one sex from the other sex, one nation or a part of it from other nations or from other parts of the same nation, one religion from other religions, one interest group from other such groups, one class from other classes, in particular the rich from the poor, the righteous from the damned and—underlying all divisiveness—one person from other persons, at work, at play so-called, in the home, in pubs and in parliaments. The horrors of separatism arise out of the notion that an individual should seek to have things his own way and groups their own way. Neither the present social scene nor the horizons of prominent personages recognize that every one functions best and suffers least as his brother's keeper.

A particularly virulent form of this conventionality settled upon the United States during the closing years of the twentieth century. Beginning as irrational objection to the payment of taxes, already the lowest among industrialized countries, it spread into a mass delusion that not alone the rich but the whole nation itself could benefit from increasing the number of poor and grinding their faces, cutting off succor from the sick, the poverty-stricken, the under-employed, and the under-educated, while slashing educational, medical, and scientific work essential to social existence.

For such delusional behavior, something deeper than simple greed, status, and oppression was at work: namely a mass confusion about the nature of reality, in the form of a defeat of factuality. Facts lost their sanctity, giving way to the ultimate dictatorship of the lie, whereby deceit gains currency simply from repetition, and where its consequences are brushed away. When human beings act as centers of the universe, when they fall prey to self projection, facts themselves become relative; they lose sanctity as things as they are.

Unless the facts of daily life, of sticks and stones, of things as they were and as they are becoming, as well as the facts of relationships between persons (for all their impenetrability): unless these facts have a reality inherent in themselves, they are useless as guides to living. People who manipulate and maneuver themselves as the center of things are delusional, often noisily so. Wholesale layoffs of workers, for example, may indeed increase the price of common stock, but the decline in the purchasing power of the downgraded worker, who is also a consumer, can lead to economic prostration, ruinous to a society that depends on mass-production not class-production. The pursuit of deceit for no more reason than the instant gratification of the rich, in the form of lower taxes and a balanced budget, is a disorder of mind and emotion: a madness. In madness lies the every-one-for-himself deceit, which throughout history has led civilizations to crash.

The madness is prevalent but not universal. Hidden in the inner recesses of human beings are traces of an utterly different and sharply opposed sense of life. In it is not only hope for the future but meaningfulness in the present; inherent in it is not an absence of suffering but an acceptance of it that leads to surcease from its agitations. It delivers from self-will, from pettiness, from aggressiveness, from supineness, in short from separateness, and leads up to wholeness and at least some measure of joy. It is not sacrosanct, but it is goodly—godly. For there is no escape from the ruinations of self unless there is a being, an entity, a totality vastly greater than self, but known by experience to be close to all living things. This entity is not comprehended or understood but experienced and felt.

The written records of such intimacy are found in accounts of the *prophetic* way of life. The early meaning of the word, and still its primary one, has nothing to do with foretelling or soothsaying; it identifies as prophets human beings who speak for Truth or are spoken through by it. And their message is not the wrath of God but the possibility of deliverance from the ruination seemingly built into the universe for civilizations that forsake Truth and cling to deceit. The prophetic is not to be defined; it is to be illustrated, particularly in terms of its current utility. Hence *The Way of the Ways*, an account of four different approaches to the prophetic that turn out to be so similar that they are one way. There are no divine manipulations: human beings are left free to make their own mistakes, hopefully to grow from them. Meanwhile God walks beside his children, shepherding them if they reach out to him, but being with them, whether they reach out or not, even suffering with them through all the tribulations of personal existence and all the horrors of human history. He is a fact of experience, in much the way that aspects of his creation are not objects of belief but experienced facts, as William James documents. God is, like his facts, inwardly and compellingly real.

The various ways provide a counterbalance to ills social as well as personal, to the world's violence, oppression, and greed. Ways of life lived luminously are the true forces of social change. They have little to do with the practices of conventional religion, given today (as so often in the past) to sacrileges, superstitions, and slaughters. Many conventional people manage to parade ostentatiously (or shyly) as reborn without having died to self-will, meanwhile shouting (or whispering) the inerrancy of dogmatic views about outward belief, whether Occidental or Oriental. But there is a Way, reflected in many distinct Ways, that can be followed; there is a Way that searches reality in its deepest aspects and finds meaning and Truth, luminously divine Truth. It is forever set against the fads, habits, and sacrileges of convention—but without being set against the human beings who are faddish and sacrilegious. In counterbalancing evil, the Way provides a totally non-violent force—the simple and compelling example of luminous lives. This Way has been followed, as the various books of this series indicate, by the prophets and their followers of Judaism, Taoism, Hinduism, Buddhism, Christianity, and Islam, all reviled and persecuted as unbelievers by the faddishly righteous.

The four books of *The Way of the Ways* are here listed but not encapsulated. The Way is not something to be informed about, but something to be absorbed and, to that end, to be read again and again. *Lao Tzŭ: TAO* is placed at the head of the series because the wit, paradox and insight of the Tao Teh Ching turn conventional knowledge upside down, showing, for example, that nothing-knowing is more useful than knowing-something. The second book in the series is *The Prophetic WORD*, an account of the prophetic writings of Judaism and Christianity, buttressed by prophetic Westerners of recent times such as George Fox and Martin Buber.

The prophets are linked together, but the linkage is inward; in no way did Lao Tzŭ and the Biblical prophets influence each other. The influence was deeper. It was as if various persons in various times and places drew from wells water whose taste differed by locality but nonetheless remained water. So it is also with the prophets of the remaining books. *John Woolman: PURE WISDOM*, Book Three has as title Woolman's term for the Way, the Light, and the Truth: the central motif of a Journal that demonstrates deliverance from self-will. Set down by no ecclesiastic but by a man of all work, it is non-creedal, non-authoritative, even non-organizational. *Gandhi: TRUTH*, the fourth book, is titled with the particular term which Mohandas Gandhi used for the divine: the word he joined with the words *simplicity* and *non-violence*, terms central to the outward work and inward life he sought for himself, for his India, and for everyone everywhere.

All these books, except the first, which is translated in full, select from the prophetic writings and in that sense edit them. But editing is a crucial need if such writings are to be allowed to speak again. Such editing as occurs in these books has been carried out for millennia, sometimes by selective memorizing, sometimes by thoughtful alterations of word and phrase. "When I come to the word enemies," says an ancient friend who has the Psalms by heart, "I read troubles. I have troubles, but I do not have enemies." This selectivity the commentator chooses to regard as deeply prophetic. Through such selectivity the Word stays alive in all its pertinence and inspiration and invites repetitive reading. To facilitate such reading, indices, notes, and sources have been placed at the end of each of the books. Acknowledgments, of which there are many, are to be found in the pages immediately following the translation.

The Way
of the Ways

Lao Tzŭ: TAO

Book One

Contents

Lao Tzŭ: TAO

Lao Tzŭ: TAO

Preface: Know Not Know

Lao Tzŭ: TAO introduces this prophetic series of books about the Way because Tao literally is the Way: Way in the sense of path, Way also in the sense of Mother of all things. Footing along the Way is more life-giving than running to the end of it. The principal early Taoist descriptions of it are available to us in the Tao Teh Ching, literally the Way Virtue Classic. Since it uncovers failure in success, fussy agitation in doing something, and perverse addiction in getting something, its title and its content sound the underlying tone of other great prophetic writings. It is a way of life, not a system of belief.

But this is to speak for the Tao Teh Ching, which speaks best for itself. It is a supremely useful introduction to prophetic writing in general, not only because Tao is literally the Way, but also because it sounds repeatedly tones heard in other prophetic works. Translated in full, it also provides a reminder that prophetic writings include varied elements of various origins, and that it is typically uneven in inspiration, consisting as it does of that which is consistently stirring, but wandering occasionally into that which is flat, that which is contradictory, and that which seems to possess no sense now discernible. *Lao Tzŭ: TAO* is, among other things, a handbook on how to read prophetic writings—all of them, not alone the Tao Teh Ching—and of how to get through the outer rind to the meat inside.

It has been necessary to translate Lao Tzŭ afresh since existing translations attempt to make him understandable. Lao Tzŭ found liberation, personal and social, in not naming things and in not cogitating theories. As a consequence, a scholarly translation of the Tao Teh Ching is somewhat contradictory in terms, but it is possible to aim at exactness. The present translation results from nearly sixty years living with the book of Tao, from the encouragement of the translator's teachers, Dr. Hu Shih and Dr. Chou Li-fei, and from sitting down with dictionaries on one side and, on the other, the translations of Dr. John C.H. Wu and Dr. Lin Yutang, which the translator admires and upon which he has drawn. The translation uses the Wang Pi text as amended in several instances by Dr. Wu in his *Lao Tzŭ / Tao Teh Ching*, New York, St. John's University Press, 1961, a revision of his "Lao Tzŭ, The Tao and Its Virtue," published in Shanghai in December 1939 in T'ien Hsia Monthly, which contains valuable commentary. The Wang Pi text, dating from the 240s A.D. but existing in manuscript form only since the 700s, has served as basis for the so-called standard text.

In 1973 two texts of much earlier date—the year 168 B.C.—were found in the village of Mawangtui in the province of Honan, and these texts, named for the village of their discovery, have stirred great philological excitement. Some four hundred years earlier than the standard text, they contain new words, new sentences, and new grammatical constructions. In 1989, they appeared in *Lao-Tzŭ, Te-Tao Ching,* by Robert G. Henricks.

The present translator has been greatly tempted to make use of the Mawangtui texts, but has kept to Wang Pi, largely because, in the words of Chuang Tzŭ, it is impossible to play two tunes at once, even though changes in meaning from the Mawangtui to the standard renditions are not major. It seems possible that the variant texts of the Tao Teh Ching so far discovered possess no common or continuing genealogy, but rather a somewhat personal, limited, and even secret character (the book was often banned) that has developed along parallel non-meeting lines. Moreover, the Tao Teh Ching, which counsels intuition rather than concept, tends to resist analysis. Until further archaeological finds define its philological character more exactly, it seems unwise to treat any one line of texts as definitive. Rather it seems wise to pursue the separate lines. In these circumstances, earlier texts do not necessarily invalidate later ones. (For discussion of these circumstances, see Appendix, p. 235.)

As for the Wang Pi version, the translator is indebted to Dr. John Wu not only for textual considerations, but also for penetrating renderings into English of the Chinese text. Parts of Chapters 29, 39, 47, 56, 64, 72, and 78 use his wording. Thanks are extended to St. John's University Press for permission for this use. Dr. Lin's annotated translation, *The Wisdom of Laotse*, New York, Random House, 1948, has been particularly helpful for its commentary. Dr. Lin is quoted in the commentary to Chapter 13, and appreciation is expressed to Random House. Appreciation for quoting the new Mawangtui texts is expressed to Ballantine Books, publishers of *Lao-Tzŭ Tao Te Ching, A New Translation Based on the Recently Discovered Ma-wang-tui Texts, Translated with an Introduction and Commentary*, by Robert G. Henricks, New York, 1989. The Tao Teh Ching, like the King James Version of the Bible, must be "translated out of the original tongues, and with the former translations diligently compared and revised."

Pronunciation Key

Pronounce Lao as if it were the last syllable of allow.
Pronounce Tzŭ as if it were Dzuh, leaving off the uh.
Pronounce Tao as if it were Dow.
Pronounce Teh as if it were Duh; *uh* should be brief.
Pronounce Ching as if it were the jing of jingle.

The curved diacritical mark over the ŭ, known as a breve, indicates that the u is to be sounded as little as possible.

Part I. The Nowness of Scripture
1.
The First
Dropout

It has become evident that conventional ways of living are culminating in an ostentation, a violence, and an oppression of the poor that, unless forsworn, can fragment life if not eliminate it. Knowledge of danger is assumed to be preventive of it, but danger grows, not because its consequences are unknown but because its roots are curiously unrecognized. Whatever may be the origins of violence in history, it is now rooted in Western man's habit of persisting in himself, existing in himself, and relating to himself whatever happens. It is shown in his telling other people what to do and, failing response, of forcing them, manipulating them, or lecturing them. It is displayed in his practice of expressing *himself*, in word and in action, in preference to expressing anything else to any other being. It is demonstrated obviously in assaults in the streets, arson in the cities, threats and skirmishes among and within the nations. It is ultimately disclosed in preparations for offensive self-defense, whereby nations, young or old, devise the termination, purposeful or more likely accidental, of vast numbers if not the whole of humanity. The danger is violence: now not so much from the world's larger nations as from its many local warlords, hankering for power not only in separatist countries but also in city slums segregated by poverty.

And it may well be that people—people counted by the head to the number of billions—are likely to be annihilated not in spite of but because of themselves. It may be that life-obliterating war is the cultural choice of men, women, and children whose inward violence (even if expressed in nothing more than contentiousness at home and competitiveness at work or, conversely, self-anger and inadequacy at both places) creates the emotional soil for world-wide plagues. Certainly there will be little peace abroad until it is made welcome at home, not only in governmental edifices but in ordinary dwellings.

For even the opposition to violence is filled with violence: the violence of people of apparent good will who know no other way of life than doing their own thing and telling other people what to do. Among such people the inward symptoms of violence often multiply: the confusion, frustration, fear, guilt, self-hate, depression, loneliness, and like distempers of men and women who are at the mercy of their unconscious minds, trained for many centuries in the contentious ways of convention. It is not that scientific finding has outstripped spiritual growth, as so often stated, but that self has dispossessed spirit and confused even the scientific understanding of reality.

Violence overcome

Tao offers another way: a way of experiencing reality and living in it. It is a way based on all of reality—all of man's being and all of nature's workings—and not on a partial reality based on willful urges to overcome other people and conquer nature. It is a way to overcome violence and oppression, both socially and personally. Perhaps it can be called *the* other way, for ways that work against violence are much the same way.

> Something there is
> Without form and complete,
> Born before heaven and earth,
> Solitary and vast,
> Standing alone without change.
> Everywhere pervading all things,
> Mothering all beneath heaven.
> I don't know its name;
> I style it Tao,
> And for want of a name call it great.

20

This one way is traced to many and diverse scriptures. It is the word as it came to Moses, to Gautama, to Isaiah, to Mohammed, to Jesus, and to many other prophets who have heard the Ultimate and have sought words to describe their hearing. Their way is actually not so difficult to follow as it is to locate, for it is not now a topic of general conversation, and there are few literary and scholarly productions in which to read about it, although conventional rationalizings abound.

Scripture unconventionalized

Sometimes the prophetic source-works seem forbidding because they are claimed as possessions by persons of moralistic and literalistic self-will, if not of violent ill will. In recent times, inspired writings about Truth have been ratiocinated out of their actual meanings into monstrous conventionalisms of a so-called religious sort. These conventionalisms have been embraced variously by militarists in Thailand when calling upon Buddha, by terrorists in Iran when seeking sanction from the Qu'ran, by Argentine gangsters when claiming Christ as a reason for torture, and by salvationist me-firsters throughout the world when claiming inerrant scriptural support for false righteousness, legalistic dogmatism, and suicidal statism. The new way of life to be found in the scriptures is to be found by an unconventional reading of them, that is, a prophetic and liberating reading, not a priestly, moralistic, and confining one. Obvious obstacles are doctrinaire veneration and self-serving misquotation, falsely called fundamentalism.

Indeed, if Westerners are ever to let their own scriptures speak to them, it may be wise to try first to understand those of other places where false familiarity and pseudo-sanctity are less likely to be barriers. It is the venture of this book about Tao—literally the *Way*—to translate and comment on a Chinese scripture that can lead to a discovery of the same Way in scriptures nearer at hand. In the life of the writer a similar venture with this same scripture, the primary work of early Taoism, led to

21

his finding the Jewish and Christian scriptures in which he
was reared and in which, quite literally, he continues to
have his being. If it be said that man is not to be inspired
by scriptures foreign to his upbringing, that none but
natives are to be saved, and that God will not listen to all
his children but only to those with a particular interpretation of particular parts of a particular scripture, then it
is necessary for those who seek the will of Truth rather
than their own will to cry sacrilege, for the offense is
against God and consists of an ultimate violence that
denies his love for his various children, his presence in
their midst, and his converse with all of them.

An anti-conventional sage

As for Lao Tzǔ, an anti-conventional sage, he can be
introduced succinctly as the first dropout. Twenty-five
hundred years ago, legend says, an old man who distrust-
ed princes, decried rituals, and disliked names dropped out
of the empire of Chou and went to live among the barbarians. He sought peace by keeping himself hidden:

> Whoever keeps to Tao
> Does not want to be full.
> Not full, he can practice
> Concealment instead of accomplishment.

He left behind a book of some five thousand characters,
called for the last two thousand years the Tao Teh
Ching—the Tao Virtue Classic—which is today as it has
long been the great sensation of Asian literature and Asian
scripture. He wrote with vividness, with starkness, with
simplicity, not without humor, and with such force that his
short work bred what is called philosophic Taoism, shaped
Buddhism, led to Ch'an and Zen meditation, created
Chinese landscape painting, influenced profoundly not so
much what was done in China as the manner in which it
was done, and served as a guidebook for persons everywhere who look for the inward power that brings inward

meaning and outward action. To Westerners this book is important not primarily because of its past effect in Asia, but because of its potential effect in a Western world that has so obviously lost its way and is trying so desperately to find a new one. Tao is *the Way* in the sense of *the path*: and the Tao Teh Ching, which appeared relatively early in the morning of historical time, describes one of a variety of paths through life that, to repeat, have always been the same Way.

Old No Names

The first fact about this particular way is that the man who wrote about it had no name. Lao Tzŭ is a description rather than an appellation. It can mean *old philosopher* or *old sir*, but it can also mean *old child* or *old fellow*. Lao Tzŭ kept himself so well hidden that very little is known of him except what he wrote. His early biographer, Ssŭ-ma Ch'ien (see Appendix), records a few titles and a few places, chronicles a chronologically impossible meeting with Confucius, and has not more of substance to report than the following:

"He was a man indeed.... In the State of Chou he was historian in charge of the secret archives....

"Lao Tzŭ practiced Tao and virtue. His teaching was the concealment of self and not having names. He lived for a long time in the State of Chou, but foreseeing its decay he dropped out and came to the frontier. The officer of the frontier was of the name Yin Hsi.

"He said, 'Sir, you are about to drop out. I urge you to write a book for me.'

"Lao Tzŭ then wrote a book of a first and second part, discussing Tao and virtue, and he wrote some five thous-and characters. Then he departed.

"No one knows where he died."

That is all. But that little could be still less without changing the impact of the book of Tao, which depends on its author *not* being known. Scholarly doubts have been expressed as to whether Lao Tzŭ lived when he is said to have lived and even whether he lived at all. But his non-existence or his existence at any time else would only dramatize his concealment of self and not having names. He is, in convention's eyes, scandalously against self.

He is also against the autocratic, the patriarchal, the hierarchic, the superstitious, the oppressive, the pretentious, and the violent. Such opposition was indeed unconventional, but it was not in itself scandalous. The completeness of Lao Tzŭ's scandal was his dropping out of Chinese civilization to live among barbarians. The dropping out was legendary, and the legend lived. It was a scandal as great to the Chinese as Hosea's taking a whore to wife was to the Israelites or as Jesus' dying the death of a criminal was to the Romans. It was, in sum, an act of unsurpassable uncouthness, a topsy-turvying of civilization. As the Jews put down temple prostitutes and as the Romans put down subversives, so did the Chinese put down the barbarians to the north and west of their country. Barbarian moral weakness was the mark of Chinese superiority. Indeed, the flight of their ancient sage to the people they looked down on remains an eternal symbol of the despicability of conventional success.

Success despicable

Martin Buber suggests that it is because of this despicability that Lao Tzŭ's teaching of following Tao and doing nothing can reach out in a living manner to Westerners as no other Asian teaching can reach out. "We have begun to learn," writes Buber, "that success is of no consequence. We have begun to doubt the significance of historical success, *i.e.*, the validity of the man who sets an end for himself, carries this end into effect, accumulates the necessary means of power and succeeds with these means of power: the typical modern Western man. I say, we begin to doubt the content of existence of this man. And there we come in contact with the teaching that genuine effecting is not interfering, not giving vent to power, but remaining within oneself.... With us this know-

ledge does not originate as wisdom but as foolishness....
But there where we stand or there where we shall soon
stand, we shall directly touch the reality for which Lao Tzŭ
spoke."

> Does anyone want to take the world
> And act on it?
> I don't see how he can succeed.
> The world is a sacred vessel
> Not to be acted on.
> Whoever acts on it spoils it;
> Whoever grasps at it loses it.

For Lao Tzŭ speaks about the joy of following a way of
life, not about the tensions of acting on the world and
chasing success or about winning a reputation and thus
making a big splash. He writes about a meeting, a relationship with Tao, with nature, with other persons, not
about obeying one or another set of precepts and persisting in them against all comers. He proposes an attitude
toward life that is full of warmth and awe, and not a
reaction against life that finds fault, assigns praise and
blame, determines guilt, and passes judgment. He demonstrates an entirely different way of thinking, one that puts
to work the entire being of man and not simply the
isolated function of cogitation which gives the illusion of
control over life. He emphasizes the Tao-given capacity
of this being to fit in with creation so long as he does not
demand that creation fit in with him—thus faulting Western egocentrism long before it came into existence.

From torment, deliverance

He does not simply castigate success and substitute for
success castigation; he demonstrates an entirely different
manner of being alive. Moreover, he promises, through the
following of the Way, a deliverance from the torments of
ego, from guilts and anxieties, rages and deceits, denials

and depressions, and from the violence and aloneness that attend the failure of success. The sage has something better to do than live for himself.

> Therefore the sage
> Puts himself last,
> Finds himself first;
> Abandons his self,
> Preserves his self.
> Is it not because he has no self
> That he is able to realize himself?

For persons brought up on counsels of achievement and self-reliance, the possibility of self-abandonment seems at first as remote as it is unwanted. The pain that success-seeking inflicts on people is typically seen by them not as something they inflict on themselves but as something inflicted upon them by external circumstances, often in the form of other competing people. By such means it is possible to self-inflict new pain to distract from old pain. For persons brought up on praise and blame, giving up guilt seems like the defeat of all law and order, since they see principles and precepts as the moral adornments of successful people, even though it is obvious that dedication to principle is characteristic of dictators and scoundrels of the sort who exist to punish those who differ from them. Indeed, a great demand of Western society, imposed alike by people of ill will and good will, is ideological purity, an inescapable consequence of trying to make self the center of the cosmos. Cogitation of the sterile and fractious sort practiced by social, scholarly, political, theological, and military dogmatists is generally held to be man's last best hope, since salvation, personal or social, is supposed to result from concepts that will control nature, society, other selves, and even one's own self. Self-will's basic urge is to control something.

The goals pursued by the will to control may be good in themselves, such as striving for peace and outlawing oppression. But so long as the conventional tools of power and will are used, so long is it impossible to achieve the good goals sought. Probably it is from the use of these conventional tools that wars and conflicts arise. The ineffectiveness of the peace movement throughout most of the twentieth century may well have resulted from its attempt to be successful in a war against war. It has been effective only when it renounced conventional tools, as did Gandhi's non-violent campaigns in India, along with the campaigns of Martin Luther King Jr., perhaps the only instances of effective group effort for peace in the twentieth century. Underlying Gandhi's testimony is the same relationship to life that underlies the book of Tao: a prophetic awareness of the spiritual reality that penetrates life, together with a realization that its power can produce changes in society that cannot be produced conventionally. Outward effort is fruitful only when it is part of a radical inward change in man's basic awareness.

This altered awareness involves new relationships with Truth, with the heavens, with earth, and with other men and women: relationships that would commonly be considered obstacles to the life of achievement, if they were to be considered at all. Indeed, the very word *relationship* is currently in process of delimitation, whereby it is becoming a circumlocution for sexual connection. In these times, most people feel themselves alone so intensely that it is difficult for them to sense the possibility of rising above clashes of will to true interaction with others. Change in established patterns of intellect and emotion appears unimaginable to most Westerners.

All things new

And yet it has been widely recognized since early in the twentieth century that these apparently immutable patterns are no more than a matter of cultural choice and not a matter of innate human condition. The human condition itself, in various living cultures throughout the world, gives evidence that man's nature is in no way rigidly fixed but rather infinitely malleable, and that a broad variety of choices is open alike to persons and peoples, particularly since the Western epoch is widely believed, at least among many historians and anthropologists, to be ending, if it not be ended already.

> Things that flourish fall into decay.
> This is not-Tao,
> And what is not-Tao soon ends.

The Bible declares the word of the everywhere God, "Behold, I make all things new." The word is not heard.

There is as yet little impetus to see the new things and to follow the new paths, even among persons who make much of their lifestyles and pursue, variously, personal meditation, communal living, political activism, sexual latitudinarianism, disordered dress, dietary rigidity, and environmental protection, or, oppositely but similarly, chemical intoxication, criminal assaults—or nationalist, separatist, terrorist, and like agitations. The dead hand of the past is as heavy upon the apparently liberated as it is upon the obviously hidebound.

Sick of sickness

For the essence of conventionality is the belief, so deeply rooted as to be largely unconscious, that the universe revolves around every single human being, that everything that happens must be related first of all to that single human being, and that meaning in life is to be found through self-expression and the assertion of self-will: activities carried out alike in self-centered anger and in the similarly self-centered conditions of doing good and being in love. Here the bomb-thrower is one with the bible-thumper, the criminal one with the righteous, the reformer one with the unreconstructed. Even the outs are one with the ins, for Western self-will is now being exported with Western technology. There is a new fervor for self-will: in recent decades egocentrists have been calling for it with the desperation of addicts clamoring precisely for drugs that kill them.

For such addictions, writings about the Way have a simple answer that goes far beyond the moralistic. Lao Tzŭ words it in this manner:

> To know and to be unknowing is best;
> Not to know and to be knowing is sickness.
> Only by being sick of our sickness
> Are we not sick.
>
> The sage is not sick.
> He is sick of his sickness
> And therefore not sick.

The answer is no different from Isaiah's counsel to turn from serving self to serving God, or from Jesus' insistence on saving one's life by losing it. But the answer cannot be heard clearly until people, everywhere or anywhere, are literally sick of their sickness: sick of trying to establish a personal self over against other selves, sick of seeking to maximize self, sick of clamoring for self-superiority or, essentially the same thing, self-inferiority: a sickness of compulsions, competitions, contests, and the consequent destruction of the true self and other selves, even to the degree of violent adventurism, psychological or physical or both.

Walking by watching

The answer is by no means unfamiliar to Westerners, for prophetic Truth has survived among them, as among most peoples, as a persistent if minor cultural theme, one customarily unnoticed but never entirely forgotten. At times Truth seems to stir in people's hearts, informing them without conscious awareness that there are such realities as meaning and affection and the very Truth itself. But it is difficult to act on such promptings if individuals try to act alone. Even when they become sick of their sickness, they seldom get well if they have not the example of other selves to follow. No self gets over self-sickness by its own self.

It is told of François de Sales that, when asked how to love God, he counter-questioned, "How does a child learn to walk?" And he explained that a child learns to walk by walking. To anybody but Westerners of do-it-yourself propensities, such a method of self-teaching would appear nonsensical. A child does not learn to walk by himself; he learns to walk by watching the people around him walk. Similarly, adults can learn to love God only by watching other people love him: or at least by watching their first steps of accepting Truth and becoming mindful of it. Since such activities are nowadays infrequent, alike among those who claim to have found God and those who claim to have found him not, they can be seen most clearly in the prophetic writings of times past.

> Why did the ancients prize the Tao?
> Because if it is sought, it is found;
> Because the guilty are forgiven.

It may be argued that contemporary thought is superior to past thought and that truth characterizes only the up-to-date. Such are the arguments of Western conventionalism. However dubious their logic, their function is to support the role of self as the center of all that exists. Whether spoken in scientific or religious terms, they speak no word concerning the violence, oppression, and pretension that erupt from self-worship—miserable alternative to the worship of the Way. They have no word to speak concerning inward torments of ego that shake the mind or with tortures of guilt that bewilder the emotions. To these things the writings of the prophets speak.

Disentangling scripture

But here it is essential to distinguish between those parts of the scriptures which record the voice of the prophets and those parts which are the work of the legalists, rulers, and priests, groups who seek to institutionalize Truth as well as conventionalize it. Such persons edit the language of the prophets, altering or confusing the original meaning. They add propositions and regulations of their own and fashion a dogmatic literature, misinterpreting or overlooking the very word they declare to be unerring—favoring instead conventional creedal constructs of right or left, and ignoring in the process the relationship between person and person, the key to man's relationship with God.

Certainly it is natural for anything so important to mankind as the scriptures to be edited, if only to make the original works comprehensible to later generations of men and women. A book that is meaningful enough to be considered inspired is bound to have been rewritten and annotated out of much of its original form (a process that is discernable in our own time in the alterations made in the writings of such men as Mohandas Gandhi and John Woolman). The language of the prophetic scriptures has to alter if its witness to that which does not alter is to retain its power. The King James Version of the Bible is a clear example of editing that does not weaken scripture's impact. What weakens it is the revisionism of publicists who temporize the changeless by explaining it: adding much of their own, overlooking much of the original, and confusing much of the rest.

The task of disentangling scripture from the revision of it is complicated by the necessity of knowing what the whole grain of the scripture is before trying to separate the chaff from it. This work is easier with a scripture foreign to one's own tradition, simply because notions of inerrant sanctity do not attach to it. The work is made still easier with the Tao Teh Ching because many later alterations made to it appear in the later and separate canonical volumes of popular Taoism, as contrasted with philosophic Taoism. Earlier alterations appear to be from the hands of Confucianists in search of reassuring conventionalities.

Physical creation and spiritual force

Explicit in the Tao Teh Ching is the sense of reality implicit in all prophetic writing, a sense that sees the penetration of physical creation by spiritual force: not the existence side-by-side of two distinct realms, but their acting together in the single realm of reality. This inter-action is beyond verbal definition to such a degree that it can also be imagined as non-action: the nothing-doing that is one of Lao Tzǔ's major themes. Indeed, Tao is into everything as well as on top of everything and certainly beyond the names used by scientists, logicians, and other dogmatists to pigeonhole reality. It is *everywhere* so much that it is far beyond legalisms, beyond rules and obser-vances, beyond morals and legislations, beyond notions of praise and blame. It is in and beyond everything; it is just everything in the same way that it is just *nothing*: the remarkable nothing that penetrates all reality from the space inside atoms and the space that supports and creates stars to that inwardness which is peculiar to mankind and which includes everything human in its very nothingness. Human beings themselves appear to be somethingness in combination with nothingness: in which mix, the some-thingness cannot exist without the nothingness. It is possible to conceptualize this nothingness but only by trivializing its immensity and its incommensurability. Nothingness often speaks directly to the inward ear, but it speaks in a way that can be described in no way by defini-tion, but only by analogy:

> Thirty spokes share one hub;
> In emptiness lies the wheel's utility.
> Kneading clay makes a pot;
> In emptiness lies the pot's utility.
> Cutting doors and windows makes a room;
> In emptiness lies the room's utility.
>
> Gain can be had from somethingness,
> But use can be had from nothingness.

In the light of such emptiness, Lao Tzŭ records a series of insights into and intimacies with the ways of creation and the ways of man. The insights are in no sense explanations of the universe; they are not ideas or myths or beliefs. They are simply glimpses of what is: they are records of experiencing what is real. Lao Tzŭ's message is not that his readers should believe in what he says in order to achieve a salvation of some sort, but rather that they should accept reality and turn to it, enjoying, as a consequence, inward well-being: a sort of spiritual hedonism in which there is joy and meaning and vitality, however much these coexist with suffering. Tao is the Way in the same manner in which God is Truth.

Like other writings of Truth, the book of Tao does not go out of date. It is genuinely open-ended, for its single witness is the reality of Tao, however Tao may manifest itself at one time or another. Set down in writing perhaps in the sixth century B.C. (again see Appendix), it is a creation of a remarkable time, for to that century belong the sayings of Gautama, Jeremiah, and Confucius. But it remains pertinent to all times simply because the Way remains the Way, just as Truth remains Truth, simplicity remains simplicity, non-violence remains non-violence, and the God of these prophetic witnesses remains the God of the prophets of all times and in all places.

> If Tao can be Taoed, it's not Tao.
> If its name can be named, it's not its name.
> Has no name: precedes heaven and earth;
> Has a name: mother of the ten thousand things....
> Mystery of mysteries, the door to inwardness.

The way of convention is to give names to all things in the universe out of a petty will to control life. The names may attach to matter or monsters, duties or deities, objects or operation, but they represent an effort to dominate reality through the agency of abstract cogitation. Lao Tzŭ disagrees. "When law and order arose," he writes, "names

33

appeared. Aren't there enough already? Is it not time to stop?" His practice and his counsel are not to name things but to be intimate with them. Truth itself is beyond name, and the name of Tao cannot be its name. Is not God—the God of all the scriptures—forever the One who is nameless and unknowable and undefined?

Paradox not really paradoxical

The opposite of naming names is creating paradoxes, and Lao Tzŭ eschews the former and embraces the latter even more fervently than do the writers of other scriptures. Sometimes mistaken for witticism or for a turning upside down of things as they are, paradox provokes insight into the awesome inexplicability of life. It is not, of course, to be defined, being hostile to names by nature. It has no laws and can be described only as it behaves: it repeats apparent opposites again and again so that the veil of words—poor indicators of a reality beyond cogitation—can be rent by the clash of apparently conflicting experiences. Paradox cuts across the accumulated thickness of language and illuminates as it cuts. It enlightens where cogitation fails. In ages of bronze or plutonium, it is the only alternative to names.

There can never be a study of it. Look at it, and you cannot see it. See it, and you will not have to look at it. Any attempt to describe it, except by paradox, leads nowhere, for it hovers somewhere just at the edge of human understanding. It is like a fleeting motion seen from the corner of the eye only when the eye is focused elsewhere. Only one definitive statement can be made about it, and that is that it is not really paradoxical. For Lao Tzŭ celebrates rather than analyzes the mysteriousness of life. He does not wonder about the universe but feels wonder toward it. He responds with awe, awe conveyed without logic through a series of affirmations of what is omnipresent both in the heavens and in the hearts of men and women and children.

Paradox is perplexing to Westerners brought up on

names. To them Lao Tzŭ can seem lacking in pertinence because he is lacking in familiarity. The commentary accompanying this translation is designed to familiarize the reader with Tao and to further his acquaintance by suggesting Tao's pertinence to his own time and place. But once the commentary has provided such introduction, it can be put aside. Hence the text itself has been printed separately, beginning on page 185. Lao Tzŭ's meaning is best assimilated by repetitive reading. Prophecy and paradox speak best for themselves.

> True words are not nice;
> Nice words are not true.
> A good man does not argue;
> An arguer is not good.
> The wise are not learned;
> The learned are not wise.

The intent of the Tao Teh Ching is to speak about the unspeakable, and, as Lao Tzŭ points out, "He who speaks does not know, and he who knows does not speak." In reading about Tao, it is well to sense the possibility and even the necessity of being intimate with a Reality that it would be presumptuous to try to comprehend. Lao Tzŭ is close to Tao with an intimacy he recommends across the ages as a new and healing reality.

Serenity and society

Let it be clear, however, that such intimacy leads to no state of benign indifference to the everyday world. Lao Tzŭ looks into the heavens to steady his feet upon the ordinary earth. Tao points not at itself but at the myriad beings who make up the human family. Lao Tzŭ's scripture is not so much about the attainment of serenity as it is about practical matters of arranging and running society. For serenity is essentially a by-product. Those who pursue it are in danger of having nightmares; those who do not may in time get a good night's sleep.

35

For the message of the prophets is not contentment; it is the following of the Way, the Truth, the divine purposiveness in all the dealings of human beings one with another. In subsequent chapters of this introduction, Lao Tzŭ will be seen in society and in history not in terms of his particular cultural locale but rather in terms of a Western locale. The answers of prophetic scripture do indeed arise out of the particularities of time and place, but they are not confined by them. The Tao Teh Ching addresses itself to frets and strains in places of work, to hostilities at home, to the pains produced everywhere by chasing success. It demonstrates how violence, inward or outward, can be overcome, even proposes a specific way to reduce ordinary crime. For all its antiquity, the text bears directly on current problems of economic productivity, obtuseness in foreign policy, and befuddlement in social and scientific research. It explores those addictions, possessions, compulsions, and ritualisms that litter the roadbed of the conventional fast lane. Later on in this book, Lao Tzŭ speaks for himself. In the next chapters, the self-concealing author of the ancient scripture of Tao is introduced by way of current malpractices.

2.
The Failure
of Success

It is the experience of Lao Tzǔ that it is natural for men, women, and children to turn to Tao, and that it is separation from Tao which is unnatural. Turning-toward is life; turning-away is death; and the choice is momentous beyond the doing of it, beyond all conventional understanding of good and evil, just as Tao itself is awesome beyond all customary descriptions of divinity and all customary methods of organizing society. Turning to Tao is not complicated; it takes up residence in all men, women and children, and answers when asked. Once there is turning-toward, there is holding-onto; and holding onto Tao is not a subject of belief and observance but of direct and factual experience, both of inward and outward reality, which Tao fuses in much the same manner as it brings together the poles of paradox into a unitary flash of insight. But the Way is more than a flash. Its light is steady. It teaches human beings even when they sleep.

> Heaven abides; earth lasts.
> They last and abide
> By not living for themselves.
> Hence they live forever.

The Way being within, it is necessary only to follow inward direction to follow Tao as heaven and earth follow. Tao has nothing to do with that celestial manipulation of man and nature wherein higher powers intervene in the normal courses of life to make special events happen or not happen. Tao is indeed the distinct and ultimate Reality toward whose completeness man, earth, and heaven move.

But it is first of all the path along which they travel. Being on the path is as life-giving as reaching the end of it, while being off the path can be spiritually death-dealing.

> If I have a grain of wisdom,
> I walk along the great Tao
> And only fear to stray.

For the Tao Teh Ching is as negative about man and the universe as it is positive (and, of course, as positive as it is negative). The misery of straying is as overwhelming as the wonder of finding. Lao Tzŭ, in common with other prophetic writers, seldom mentions the one condition without implying at least the other. Indeed, the one seems to come from the other, since moving toward Tao is typically a consequence of having gone away. In trying to take in the Tao Teh Ching, it is important to avoid explaining any element of it intellectually and conceptually, since all elements of it emphasize an experience of life that is inherently non-conceptual. Reason here helps understanding when not allowed to dominate it. Let it be said simply (and insufficiently) that people are driven to the comfort of health by the pain of sickness.

Self-will sick

The first impact, therefore, of the Tao Teh Ching is negative even in its positive passages—or particularly in such passages. How sick sick people are!

> On tiptoe you don't stand.
> Astride you don't walk.
> Showing yourself, you don't shine.
> Asserting yourself, you don't show.
> Boasting yourself won't get you credit.
> Vaunting yourself won't let you endure.
>
> In Tao, these things are called
> Tumors and dregs, which all things abhor.
> Whoever has Tao does not dwell on them.

38

When the Tao Teh Ching is used as a critique of our contemporary time of troubles, it is evident that the troubles result not from a series of particular ills but from an attitude toward reality, whereby people desert Tao and try to find meaning and motivation in their own selves or, by self-projection, within their own groups, which enhance the value of self by devaluing outsiders. Indeed, man's false view of himself, in which he sees himself as the center of the universe, is the key not only to Lao Tzŭ's denunciation of success but also to his praise of Tao. If a man does not follow Tao, or in Western terms worship the Truth which is God, he will have little to follow and nothing to worship but himself. The deceit of this idolatry is so pernicious that it becomes the sickness of sicknesses. Other ailments of opulence, oppression, and violence, whether expressed in hatred of others and a will to dominate or in self-hatred and a will to be injured, spring from this central deceit.

In Western terms, a positive response to such deceit is to love and do as you please. Lao Tzŭ says:

> Twist and get whole.
> Bend and get straight.
> Be empty and get filled.
> Be worn and get renewed.
> Have little: get much.
> Have much: get baffled.
>
> Therefore,...
> [The sage] does not show himself,
> Hence he shines;
> Does not assert himself,
> Hence he is seen;
> Does not boast his merits,
> Hence he gets credit;
> Does not vaunt himself,
> Hence he survives;
> Does not compete with anyone,

Hence no one beneath heaven
Can compete with him.

The old saying,
The twisted shall be made whole,
Is no empty phrase.
Be whole and you will return.

This counsel of wholeness can indeed be followed in times of noises and alarms, but it is not a prescription for self-discovery or self-fulfillment. Nor is Lao Tzŭ a mystic in the sense of taking people out of this world to cling to a supermundane deity. Rather, Lao Tzŭ sees the reality by which men and women, consciously and unconsciously, live their daily lives as the primary force that energizes the world of outward history. Change the world, you do not thereby change man, and you therefore make no more than superficial changes in the world. Change man, whom Tao makes infinitely malleable, you change the world.

But there is no change, individual or social, until men and women are sick enough of self-will to recognize what they are sick with. Otherwise self-will is dismissed as something other people alone are sick with. Yet even in matters of apparent triviality like the weather, it is everywhere epidemic. The rain, for instance, rains first of all on me. It is so personal to me that I am in a perverse relationship to it, so that it will fall if I don't carry an umbrella, hold off if I do: a line of reasoning I recognize to be slightly ridiculous—thousands of other persons are reasoning in the same way—but one which I am willing to own to even publicly, with suitably wry humor, out of simple but satisfying self-gratification.

Denigration at work

At places of work, shop politics are commonly held to be the work of people of unusually self-centered will. And yet men and women recognize from their own acquaintance with triumph and failure that they themselves, no less than others, use workplaces to measure themselves against other selves. Their lives, like the mirrors in restrooms, have been arranged for purposes of competitive comparison. People seek the status of telling other people what to do, try to avoid the non-status of being told. When possible, they denigrate the labor of others, if only to themselves, in favor of their own. They show off. They gossip. They constantly compare. They conspire to get themselves recognized and others over-looked. Unless, of course, they seek the enticements of low ego, whereby self-will feeds on self-denigration.

Indeed, it makes little difference whether men and wo-men assert or deprecate themselves, so long as attention is focused on themselves, whether they be sublimely con-fident or miserably depressed. Nothing focuses attention more forcefully on self than a state of guilt, misery, and general inadequacy. Establishing supremacy often fails, but establishing inferiority always succeeds. Deceits of this sort lead men and women to interpose compulsions and evasions and escapes, not to mention fantasies and denigrations and combats, between themselves and reality: to such a degree, indeed, that it is difficult to distinguish fact from self-will, a state of affairs hardly conducive to work or play.

This situation is the reverse of Lao Tzŭ's saying:

> [The sage] does not compete with anyone,
> Hence no one beneath heaven can compete with him.

Restated for current times, the couplet would read:

> Because you want to compete with everyone,
> All beneath heaven will compete with you.

The consequence is not simply competition but also hos-tility compounded with fear. Places of work more and more become courts of judgment for testing one person against another, arenas for winning sympathy or nursing

41

inferiority, and theaters of hidden conflict and innuendo, in which it is necessary to guard against slurs, threats, reprimands, cabals, and warnings. The enormity of the hidden hostility that pervades offices, factories, and schools—competition-teaching centers—is widely overlooked because most people choose not to see beyond the injustices with which they are personally visited. Beyond personal hurt lies a system of semi-organized hostility, in which exists open approval of aggressive self-serving with no economic or pedagogical justification. Office politics apart, large enterprise, whether commercial or educational, actually functions on the basis of cooperation, not competition, yet work and school are occasions to pit self against self.

Such encounters are generally known to be confusing, painful, and exhausting. Yet people still insist on being treated well while they dream of other people being treated ill, an insistence that simply intensifies the encounter. Often hostility rises no higher in intensity than is required to judge others, but not infrequently it erupts in anger and reveals itself to be an overwhelming urge (not simply a device) to achieve superiority or to reinforce inferiority or to do both at once, but above all a simple drive to give expression to self, even if the self be alone, withdrawn, and miserable.

Nothing beneath heaven
Is softer and weaker than water.
Nothing is better
To attack the hard and strong,
And nothing can take its place.
The weak overcome the strong;
The soft overcome the hard.

There is no one beneath heaven
Who doesn't know this,
And no one who practices it....
Indeed straight words seem crooked!

If, again negatively, we examine ourselves at home, we see a hostility that forces us to defame the people with whom we live rather than admit our own self-sickness: nothing is wrong with us; something is wrong with, say, the family or at least particular members of it. Men and women seek closeness: find aloofness; they wish to give love and receive it: often settle for no more than the narcissistic self-projection familiarly known as being in love. Too closed to receive and too shackled to give affection, they attempt to be recipients of their own love: a hopeless try since it is futile to receive without giving and impossible to give to self without having given selflessly to others.

"All we like hens have gone astray"

Without mutuality, a household can come to resemble not so much the barnyard—cattle, sheep, and pigs at least huddle and wallow together—as the chicken coop, where separate individuals busy themselves pecking and being pecked. Who shall cluck at whom? What shall strut in front of what? Such questions are settled not by an inward look at self-sickness but by projecting self-sickness into group life, and the answer is proclaimed that something outside self is wrong, in particular that ancient device of mutual aid, the family.

The will to undercut one's spouse, to enlarge gaps between generations, to dominate one's children, to get even with one's parents, deceiving the old and training the young in new deceits (when not actually abusing them), using humor to cut at others, playing roles of consequence in the lives of persons nearby, and from time to time contending with and gossiping about other human group-ings: all this hen-like hostility is tolerated without realizing that it is inhuman. Indeed, all the pettiness and tawdriness and miserable ineptitude of self-will is so con-trary to humanity that any human being can give it up without undue difficulty whenever he is willing to do so. "Abandon righteousness," advises Lao Tzŭ, "and the people will go back to natural affection." Righteous self-love is not at all natural; ordinary humble goodness is. While interchange between family members survives, at least as a means of vocalizing hostilities, conversation as the ancient mainstay of household pleasure has given way to solitary pursuits, in particular the watching of television, which appears to be the cultural choice of a people who have decided that dialogue must at all costs be killed. More and more people eat separately and watch television together. It is only incidentally the function of that medium to tell lies, stimulate fears, enthrall with violence, and besot the emotions. Its prime function is simply to keep people watching itself, to which end it stirs the fears and tensions that feed a projected sense of self. It is itself a projected self, one that makes it difficult to do anything at home other than ward off reality and savor the artificial spice of manufactured anxiety and canned hostility.

Hostility in the bedchamber

Hostility nowadays is said to have invaded the bedchamber, where affection was long believed to prevail. Some three hundred years ago, in a pamphlet pleading against judicial cruelty and religious intolerance, William Penn wrote, "Nothing but kindness keeps up the human race. Men and women don't get children in spite of but because of affection. 'Tis wonderful to think by what friendly and gentle ways nature produces and matures the creatures of this world." We are now informed by not a few students of the emotions that hostility is more important in the sexual act than affection. Until the spread of the acquired immune deficiency disease, the public was being informed by not a few professional researchers in eroticism that sex needs enhancing by group activities practiced sequentially or simultaneously. And the public is still assured by supposed authorities that solitary sex is more gratifying than partner sex.

How much sexual latitudinarianism has increased in incidence is unknown, but the publicity given to it suggests

44

that fascination with it has increased considerably. It would seem that there may well be a growing preference, in fantasy at least, for sex with unknown persons, who excite because of unfamiliarity, over sex with known persons for whom human emotions can be felt. Preference of such sort suggests hostility widely felt. The various forms of less-than-social sex are gratifying to persons who want to interact with themselves, and who thus perpetuate the anti-eroticism that has so very long characterized Western civilization, the conventions of which hold that people are supposed to be splendidly alone and not close to one another.

Ecstatic self and miserable self

Happily, people are not what they are supposed to be. But neither are they what they are capable of being. While most men and women have unconscious acquaintance with the Way sufficient to make them shun drastic departures from it, they generally remain blind to the deep lodgment of hostility and willfulness and fear within them. Men and women have really only two alternatives: to follow the Way or not to follow it. To follow it somewhat more than persons who actively shun it, as do people who dislike outward violence and selfishness, may harm fewer people but does little to increase inward well-being or decrease social evil. Ordinary egocentrics are not less miserable than extreme ones, and their misery is no less contagious. Inward misery and social disorder, be it remembered, are consequences of straying from Tao.

Of those who actively shun Tao, Lao Tzŭ says:

> The great Tao is easy indeed,
> But the people choose by-paths.
> The court is very resplendent;
> But very weedy are the fields
> And the granaries very empty.
> They wear gaudy clothes,
> Carry sharp swords,

45

Exceed in eating and drinking,
Have more riches than they can use.
Call them robber-braggarts:
They are anti-Tao indeed!

This denunciation hits at the people in any epoch, not
alone the early Chinese epoch, who are autocratic, competitive, oppressive, self-conscious, class-conscious, superstitious, deceitful, and violent. But the denunciation
extends also to those persons who are opposed precisely to
these characteristics. Interposing good causes between
oneself and Tao is not much different in its inward effects
from interposing bad causes. In our days of compulsively
neurotic interposition, those who chase after good causes
are probably more numerous than those who chase after
bad ones. One measure of the inward crises that grip so
many people is the failure of good-intending and self-
intending individuals to find emotional comfort in their
causes, whatever their nature and however intently they
are pursued.

Indeed, the search for self—whether the ecstatic self or
the miserable self—distracts attention from the true path
along which such good things as justice and peace are to
be found, and it breeds, when they are not found, fear,
rage, guilt, depression, aloneness, alienation, and deceit.
Even when the self becomes dubious about success on
individual terms and seeks it in dedication to gurus and
groups, it still follows its failed fantasies and frustrations
and resentments and competitions and compulsions. The
mind is set to work to keep reality away and, mindless of
its own devices, is left at the mercy of unconscious
posturings.

When Tao is lost, there is virtue.
When virtue is lost, there is humanity.
When humanity is lost, there is morality.
When morality is lost, there is ceremony.
Now ceremony is the shell of

Loyalty and trust
And the beginning of befuddlement.

For what is less than Tao is not more than befuddlement.

In the pursuit of good ends, success fails not alone because means and ends are out of harmony but because the inward drive that underlies both means and ends is out of harmony with life, with Tao. The very notion of success, in the sense of gathering power for a good purpose and using it to achieve that purpose, means more often than not the failure of the good purpose. When success is sought consciously only as a means, it is usually sought unconsciously as an end: as, for instance, in taking intellectual stances or moral positions that serve as secret advertisements for one's self. The power that is sought to make these positions prevail is not so much the power to get things done as it is to tell other people what to do, not so much for making other people free as for making them obliged to do what is thought good for them, not so much for casting down unrighteousness as for displaying self-righteousness. When other persons try to foist intellectual, social, or moral convictions upon a person, he sees their hidden motivations clearly. When he does the same, he fails to see even the foisting.

The fascination with power among men and women of liberal intention lies in the fact that power is the act of impressing one's own will or the will of one's own group on others, whether the issues be large ones of state or small ones of daily life. An obvious ploy is manipulating children to act affectionately instead of demonstrating how to go about being affectionate in one's own life. When affection fails at home, just as when peace fails abroad, the answer is more power. Few peace-making parents are alert to their tyranny over their offspring.

"Seekest thou great things? Seek them not"

Suppose, for example, that I have convictions on the subject of peace. I am stricken by the possibility of atomic

conflagration and convinced that it is increased by arma-
ments and threats of war. To help break the chain of violence that links one war to the next, I insist publicly that a
mental analysis of violence bred by violence be accepted
by enough people to force others in power to change their
minds. Therefore I argue strenuously for my understanding of history, current events, and future projections. I
undertake to gather large crowds of marching and shouting demonstrators, and try to win publicity for them,
hopefully television publicity. I parade with colorful signs
and striking costumes. I orate with emotion. I call names.
I demonstrate. I stir fear. I tell other people what to do. But
other people, precisely the other people whose minds I
seek to alter, see clearly that what I am really seeking is
the power to become a celebrity, an authority figure, and a
self-righteous prig who knows what is good for other
people and is simply going to put the other people down in
order to control them. Lao Tzǔ writes:

> Give up wisdom, abandon knowledge,
> And the people will benefit a hundredfold.
> Give up benevolence, abandon righteousness,
> And the people will go back to natural
>   affection.
> Give up cunning, abandon gain,
> And robbers and thieves will disappear.

In self-righteousness lies the final failure of success.
The call of all the prophetic teachers is for goodness, but
when goodness is measured against the goodness of other
persons, it ceases to be good and becomes divisive and
self-serving. Faced with such alternatives, the true prophets choose not to succeed. They fail not alone in worldly terms, but even in terms of their goal of turning people
to Truth. Their true victories, which belong not to them but
to Truth itself, arise out of their repeated failures. Moses
emerges as an awesome teacher, not in spite of but

48

because of the series of repeated setbacks he suffers tragically in the midst of the desert wanderings as he tries to lead the people to a new sense of God; and at the very end of the wandering he fails even to gain entry into the promised land. Jeremiah cries out, "Seekest thou great things? Seek them not," and finds himself outcast by men who "oppress and oppress, deceive and deceive." Gautama was so much a failure that he turned his back on his own courts and palaces. And Jesus, who aimed his teaching at the poor and unlettered, spoke with harshness of the self-righteous and was so little a success that he suffered the opprobrious death of a criminal.

Success rejected

Himself a dropout and probably a castoff, Lao Tzŭ too rejected success and found, in common with other teachers like him, victory in the simple reality of the Way, the Way by which man can be healed inwardly in his dealings with others and outwardly through his realization of it, however partially, in the outward world. Once the Way is sensed, things inward and outward fit readily into a place that is recognized to be right, even though in outward conventional life there still is no such place. Men and women look within themselves and look outside themselves, and in both directions they see purpose and direction and meaning.

Perhaps this is a victory that can come to every person who learns to know the failure of success. When Truth is shunned, men and women look within themselves and find little more than a meaninglessness they try vainly to overcome through self-awareness, consciousness-raising, and other egocentric stirrings that prompt them to seek emotional as well as material success. Primarily their search is a search for meaning, for something that will justify them in their lives and confirm them in their beings. But when the search leads to a power over others that can be supported only by the illusion of self-righteousness, then the attractiveness of success is seen—

or begun to be seen—as illusion. Next it is seen as danger. Thus seen, success itself abruptly fails; and unless the search for distinction is given up, a search must be started elsewhere. Peculiarly alluring in these circumstances is personal and civic righteousness, but this cloak—worn on top of success and failure, praise and blame, by people who are trying to hide the tawdriness of their under-garments—soon unravels. The collapse is salutary, for out of its torments there can come a new attitude toward life and a new way of it.

> The great Tao flows everywhere;
> It can go to the right or the left.
> The ten thousand things draw life from it,
> And it does not deny them.
>
> It completes its work
> But takes no title.
> It clothes and feeds the ten thousand things,
> But does not own them.
> You can call it small.
> The ten thousand things return to it,
> But it does not own them.
> You can call it great.
>
> Because it does not seek to be great
> Its greatness is accomplished.

3.
Nothing-
Doing

The alternative to success is *nothing-doing*, not a negative restraint or a holding back from life, but a moving forward and a reaching out to the beyond-words reality of Truth. Nothing-doing is actually a way of getting things done; it is also a way of doing them with a vigor and completeness that result from following the Way. It is not an upside-down bit of humor. Lao Tzŭ says flatly:

> Do nothing-doing
> And everything will get done.

In Chinese, the very character for action is said to reflect distaste for fussy interference with life. Some commentators observe that its ancient form appears to derive from a representation of a man trying to pull an elephant around by the nose. But that was long before it fell victim to something-doing Communism and something-doing Capitalism.

Nothing-doing means more than simply avoiding interference. It means, negatively, not projecting self as the center of all that happens, not impressing one's will on events, not manipulating people and things, not devising grandiose plans or intricate sequences of plans, and, simply, not combating other people, not violating nature, not destroying things, not murdering others. *Something-doing*, which to Lao Tzŭ is virtually synonymous with violence, comes from self-will, which is false to the Way, false to nature, false to the nature of humankind.

Positively, nothing-doing means something so profound and vital that it is beyond talking about. It is inherent in the inward-outward reality of Tao that pervades all things

51

and all beings, that makes events fruitful by not chan-
neling them but by freeing them: the reality that creates
history not out of the decisions of a controlling few, but out
of the thoughts and actions of the many. Nothing-doing
even provides a telling means of communication whereby
what a person is and does speaks louder than what he says.
In the long run, nothing-doing always wins over
something-doing, but its workings are best described by
analogy with soft things like water which wear away
all hardness.

> The softest things beneath heaven
> Overcome the hardest.
> Nothingness alone penetrates no-space.
> Hence I know the use of nothing-doing.

Unnatural violence

Thus, in innumerable avenues of life, nothing-doing
means acceptance instead of attachment, ease instead of
discomfort. It is one of three principal ways of turning to
Tao (nothing-knowing and nothing-wanting are the other
two); it is like the other two in healing the sick and re-
storing the weary. But nothing-doing is like them also in
decrying conventional seductions that promise fun and
glitter and deliver darkness and pain. Acceptance of life is
not to be had until the seductions of life as it is not are cast
aside. They are not natural to humankind, insists Lao Tzŭ,
but unnatural. They are against Tao, in particular the
seductions of violence, whether physical or psychological.
Violence, so enticing and so threatening for contemporary
people, can lose its deadly emotional grip in the light of
the reality of nothing-doing.

In the something-doing and often patriarchal West, that
which is natural is held suspect, for it is believed that it is
natural for nature to be violent and natural for man to lie,
steal, and kill. Hence man is to be prevented from following his "natural" urges by systems of praise and blame,
reward and punishment, manipulation and restraint. Personal violence can be overcome, it is believed, only by

organized violence; and it is believed further that this organized violence has civilized man and brought him out of a savagery in which he is supposed by inclination to have assaulted, raped, or robbed whomever he met. This comic-strip view of man as a club-wielding animal, dragging women about by the hair, would be amusing did it not coincide with popular (and, for a long time, philosophical and anthropological) views of savagery as something that contemporary man has had to rise above through the agencies of churches, courts, and prisons.

Such a view is witness to the pathetic attempt of Western egocentrics to cloak themselves in the garments of righteousness. Stone-age people, who were still the common people of the bronze-age times in which Lao Tzǔ wrote, were an essentially simple (and essentially matrilocal) people, incapable of projecting self as the center of all that happens. Recent research into prehistory in China suggests them to have been remarkably free of wars and oppressions. They seem to have been dependent on and delighted by daily sustenance, ordinary quiet, family conversation, and common affection, as are not a few country peoples, hill peoples, island peoples, and rainforest peoples still alive today. To be sure, they were undoubtedly very dirty, diseased, short-lived, and highly superstitious. Undoubtedly they gave way at times to theft, violence, and other forms of selfishness. But they did not organize theft and violence into a manner of living, and they knew little of the neurotic involvements of self-will. Indeed, it is from these simpler patterns of living (the source perhaps of Golden Age legendry) that men and women may well have learned the Way, while it is from the far different patterns of the ages of bronze and iron that they may have developed notions of patriarchal honor, organized violence, and self-willed deceit.

Violence disorganizes

Of the prophetic voices raised against such violence, Lao Tzǔ, a man of the Bronze Age, is one of the earliest:

53

He who uses Tao to guide rulers
Does not force beneath-heaven with arms.
Such things recoil on their users.

Where armies are
Briars and brambles grow.
Bad harvests follow big wars.
Be firm and that is all:
Dare not rely on force.
Be firm and not haughty,
Firm but not boastful,
Firm but not proud,
Firm but non-violent....

What others have taught, I also teach:
Men of violence perish by it.
Whoever said this is father of my teaching.

What have this teacher—and his teacher—to say to-day? Let us create in caricature a current man of violence for Lao Tzŭ's inspection. This new man sees disaster as the consequence of the outward violence that other men perpetuate, and not as the consequence of the inward violence that he practices unawares himself. He is fascinated with internecine adventurism of the Iran-Contra and Yugoslav sorts, not to mention the Somalian foray and the mighty invasions of wicked countries. He amuses himself with wildly romantic spy stories and science fiction of improbable but egocentric bent. He delights in details of violent conspiracies which he holds to be rife. And he is stirred by the contemporary equivalent of saber-rattling, which includes nonsensical talk about the tactical use of instruments of annihilation and about survival through their employment. Something-doing can produce marked headiness of emotion. The new man of violence can experience the bravura of threats and declamations and can thrill to the luxuriant adrenalism of fear and anger, and precisely at the same time can strongly oppose outward war in his own mind: as indeed does practically everyone of minimal sanity today, not excluding the professional military.

Only he never observes to himself what is obvious to himself (and to practically everyone of every shade of political opinion): that the nation-state as Westerners have known it for half a millennium is suddenly at an end. It cannot make its will prevail internationally—even after the Russian cave-in—and cannot protect its citizens or advance its interests or secure its sources of raw materials, without in effect chancing national suicide. While horse-riding rulers can still indulge in brief military adventures, the nation-state of yesterday is possible today only for a few emerging third-world countries who remain able to fight among themselves—or threaten to fight—openly, secretly, or terroristically. Yet the nation-state itself is not publicly recognized as a dead end, and the urgency of finding other instruments to take its place is seldom felt and never acted on. Centuries of something-doing have resulted in nothing done, and it has taken an ancient sage to help us see it.

Violence a drug

An important use of the Tao Teh Ching is to help Westerners recognize the hidden attraction to violence that makes them blind to the most ordinary and obvious dangers of it, ranging from self-destruction to universal annihilation and including such hapless adventures as the rescue raid in Iran in the seventies, the arms-hostage-contra swaps in the eighties, and excursions into Iraq and Central America in the nineties. Rooted in the self-worship of me-first egocentrism, outward violence emerges out of fear that is stirred by the combative atmosphere of daily living, even of daily playing. Contemporary amusements are steeped in anxiety and shot through with conflict, as shown in sports, advertisements, soap operas, television dramas, horror movies, war-to-be movies, suspense stories supposed to be comic, murder stories supposed to be more entertaining than love stories, and the new fiction and non-fiction that celebrate violence commingled with sex and hate. Nature shows on television give heavy emphasis to the fearfulness of animals being eaten by animals, and news programs exhibit a propensity for displaying dead and dismembered bodies, taboo for countless centuries during which violence occurred only off stage. It is impossible to have emotions played up and down upon by such dubious entertainment without losing the feeling that violence is evil and that there is such a thing as physical and spiritual reality. Violence intoxicates; indeed, its very nature is toxic.

Crime promotion

The fear and violence of crime are not dissimilar from the fear and violence of war. They attract, they fascinate, they preoccupy: not simply those persons who are actively involved but also those who appear to be passive onlookers. Lao Tzŭ intimates that the two groups are indeed psychologically linked.

> When people are hard to govern,
> Their rulers are something-doing.
> That is why they are hard to govern.

That is to say, the poor commit crime partly because the rich not only expect them to but also, perversely, want them to: a perversity still common today. Wanted, more or less consciously, by dominant groups is a social system that rewards rapacity while providing obstacles to being raped, and that at the same time permits rape sufficient to keep people generally athrill with fear, violence, and self-righteousness—a condition possible only when the righteous have the unrighteous to cluck their tongues at. For what is better to cluck at than muggings and stabbings and rapings? The crime of punishment, writes psychiatrist Karl Menninger in his book of that title, is precisely this self-righteousness admixed with hidden guilt over secret un-

56

righteousness. Small wonder that crime provides the principal content of newspapers and television programs. In contemporary social systems, bottom-drawer people serve to justify top-drawer people in their position, and criminals are everywhere considered the lowest people in the bottom drawer. Besides, they are misapprehended as including other groups of outcasts, including people of color, who, by being thought criminal, can be treated as non-people.

Other dramas of immorality incite to crime, notably the conspicuous consumption and pretension of people who win notoriety for their something-doing, success-involved selves. The actuality of violence in the home and on the streets arises in considerable part from a desire somehow to imitate such egocentrism and to show superiority over other people if only by mugging or killing. (War itself is a device used to demonstrate such superiority.) Crime nowadays reflects less the material plight of the necessitous (badly supplied with goods but probably less badly than at previous times in history), and more the will of the underdog to have his self gratified, or at the very least exercised, as effectively as the overdog's. As a criminal motive, self-expression has now more push than has cupidity.

The lure of criminality

Defacing nature, destroying property, thieving goods, setting fire to cities (the very cities to which people flocked for more than seven centuries to find new life and a new culture): these are essentially devices for self-assertion and for establishing oneself as a something instead of a nothing. Street drugs stimulate riotous self-will; the consequent assaults are carried out less for money than for ego. Thus mugging and murder, in which victor directly confronts victim, are dramatic acts to establish superiority; even if the victor is caught or killed, he may well appear on television, thought to be the pinnacle of recognition. Murder has become what Hobbes declared it to be, the ultimate equalizer. Nothing more grotesquely illustrates the intoxication of success, the inward swagger of it, the upthrust of physical sensation, the flooding of adrenaline, the bloodrush of conquest.

Emotions experienced by the criminal can be experienced vicariously by those who only imagine they will be among his victims. Compelling are those visceral sensations stirred by fascination for violence when admixed with fear of it. This fascination, indeed, seems also to be a matter of cultural choice. In effect, people prefer high rates of criminality because their egos demand regular doses of the something-doing of daily violence. Thus prisons overflow and the rate of crime goes up until society seems to be unable to protect itself. Society wants crime; the people who make up society demand it, so that efforts to decrease crime usually multiply it. Even democratic countries have increased so greatly the volume of their laws and the size of their legal and penal systems that their criminal controls far exceed those of any of the ancient oriental despotisms. Lao Tzŭ says:

> The more laws and orders there are,
> The more thieves and robbers appear.
> Therefore the sage says:
> I do nothing, and the people of themselves reform.

For Westerners, it is more attractive to do something. A sharp reduction in current crime could be effected almost overnight by state sale rather than gangster sale of drugs to addicts, but this alternative is held to be an unrighteous coddling of outcasts, while the idea of discouraging crime by discouraging use of legal drugs like alcohol (a factor in probably a majority of all crimes) is dismissed out of hand. It would seem that people who are not themselves criminal insist on living in such a way that there is no way *not* to have criminals.

There is another way

No different from the pretenses of robbers and murderers are the practices of self-supported terrorists and self-directed revolutionaries who believe that eggs should be broken Lenin-like to make omelets according to their recipes. Not for them is the prophetic way:

> If you don't exalt the worthy:
> People then will not compete.
> If you don't prize rare goods:
> People then will not steal.
> If you don't show what is covetable:
> The people's hearts won't be upset....
> [The sage] leads the people
> To not-know and not-want,
> And the cunning ones to dare not do.
> By doing nothing-doing,
> Everything gets done.

This prophetic way (it is, to repeat, also the way of such teachers as Isaiah, Gautama, and Jesus) is specifically denounced by slaughterers who believe their good causes give them a specific license to kill. Conspiracies of misguided violence have long been a romantic attraction to Westerners who want to grasp the world and mold it to their own image, at the personal sacrifice of love, life, liberty, and even common honesty. Attempts of this sort at social change are so weighted with the conventionalism of self and violence that very little change can take place. What usually takes place is not much more than wretched criminality. Filled with awe for themselves alone, the terrorists, the ultranationalists, the separatists, and other dividers of people escalate their emotions with a frenzied bloodletting, describable only as utter nihilism. Striking sparks in a dynamite factory can hardly be progressive. Indeed, nothing can any longer be imagined to be as reactionary as violence, along with the something-doing that is the basis for it. For the problem goes beyond terrorism to the absorption in evil of people who want to impress their self-will on the world. This something-doing infects not only the terrorist but the street punk, not only the punk but the citizen who from time to time dreams of gore. But there is Tao:

> Tao never does anything,
> And everything gets done.
> If a ruler can keep to it,
> The ten thousand things
> Will change of themselves....
>
> Nature speaks little.
> Squalls do not last the morning
> Nor downpours the day.
> What stirs them up?
> Heaven-and-earth!
> Even heaven-and-earth
> Does not long make a fuss.
> How much less should men!

The Way operates in all aspects of life, personal and social. How it operates is a futile question. The Way is something to walk on and nothing to cogitate about. For nothing-knowing, says Lao Tzŭ, is a key part of nothing-doing. And that is another chapter.

4.
Nothing-
Knowing

Just as the fussiness of something-doing leads Lao Tzŭ to uphold nothing-doing, so does the fuzziness of something-knowing lead him to applaud nothing-knowing, which is an emptiness of mind akin to the selflessness of speech in his famous quotation, "He who knows does not speak; he who speaks does not know." Nothing-knowing has to do with more than self. It is a key to the ultimate nothingness. It has to do with creation, how it is everything and how its nothingness may be experienced.

> Do nothing-doing;
> Manage nothing-managing;
> Taste nothing-tasting.
> Exalt the low; multiply the few;
> Repay hatred with virtue.

His strong affirmations stress acceptance of whatever life brings; his counsel of neighborliness reaches heights of good will. Then his counsel becomes personally offensive: "Give up learning and you will have no anxieties." And he bitingly contrasts the hopeful condition of "stupid stupid" with the hopeless condition of "clever clever." To most Western scholars, such language suggests distaste for the edifices of intellect they inhabit, and it is conventional for many of those who know about the Tao Teh Ching to dismiss it as mystical and quietist and mindlessly subjective. And yet it is not mystical in the sense of seeking absorption in the All; nor is it quietist in the sense of withdrawing from the here and now. Written in the form of a handbook on how to govern (possibly because those who governed were then the only people who knew how to read), it is intensely social in its purposes and dedicated firmly to the well-being of commoners, not the power of rulers. The book, moreover, is obdurately factual. Lao Tzŭ treats *what is* as inviolate, avoids subjectivity, and turns his back ahead of time on the superstitions popular Taoism later embraced. Subjectivity and superstition result from relating reality to one's own self and trying to control it, while factuality results from relating to Tao and avoiding any effort to control anything.

Reality without seams

The Tao of Lao Tzŭ is reality without seams, with no separations of any sort between observable fact and inward fact, both so commingled in the wholeness of Tao as to have no separate significance. It *is* whole. It is not a patchwork of diverse theories that try to explain the universe and make it intelligible to limited intellects.

But to reason thus is to turn an introduction of Lao Tzŭ into a cogitation about him. The book of Tao, like Tao itself, is to be known by nothing-knowing, by being open to it, by absorbing it, by becoming intimate with it, not by building mental constructs on top of it.

> Without going out of the door
> You can know beneath-heaven.
> Without looking out of the window
> You can see heaven's way.
> The farther you go,
> The less you know.
>
> Thus the sage
> Knows without walking,
> Sees without looking,
> And does without doing.

Such is the wholeness of Tao, unseen by the self centered on self. Unless there be that wholeness, unless there be

Tao or Truth or whatever other designation shall be given to undivided Reality, then absoluteness of fact is only too easily compromised by the egocentrism of the observer. Indeed, the Tao Teh Ching penetrates sharply into the confusions of what much later became the Faustian way of thinking. However remarkable may be the results of logic and science in the realm of inventiveness, in the realm of actuality the method we call scientific can be vitiated by the will to control nature through understanding it, conceptualizing it, cogitating it, cutting it down to human size, and subjecting it to the operations of one aspect of man's being, his intellect. Knowledge is thus given an ego spin, to the extent that it sometimes twirls so far off into areas of simplification and personalization that no knowledge at all results. This chapter looks at such twirlings as they occur in high places of intellect, as for instance, scientific research, medical nomenclature, and economic manipulation. In such places, ignorance may indeed be socially as well as personally far more fruitful than cleverness.

Deceit, covert and overt

In scientific research, remarkable departures from factuality have been chronicled for more than two generations by students of the history of ideas. The consequences include arguing ahead of solid facts, elaborating theories on the basis of limited facts, treating a tool like mathematics not as a tool but as a fact, assuming that facts too distant to be examined are structured the same as facts closer at hand, and imposing unconscious personal imaginings upon factual reality.

Projection of this sort may be nothing more than an attempt of a conventional sort to explain nature. But it may also be gross deceit in the form of misstatement of fact, and it may be made, as even the daily newspapers have reported, to further entirely personal interests. Reported have been frauds in biological and psychological research. Indeed, the frequency of fraud appears to be increasing. In some cases, the intention to deceive is hidden, statistical manipulations being used, sometimes unconsciously, to make the data prove what the investigator started out to prove. But in other cases, the raw data themselves are falsified. Deceit of this sort is a particular form of self-deceit. If I hold that facts are not sacred, I can find myself at the mercy of the notion that the universe is not meaningful but that I am, and that I can make of everything precisely what I will. *I will* takes precedence over *it is*. It is difficult to be in a relationship with even simple everyday facts without being in a relationship to an ultimate Truth from which a fact emerges to be exactly as it is. The egocentric choice is to gather more and more data and have it pertain less and less to anything beyond self. Hence:

> To get learning, add to it daily.
> To get Tao, subtract daily.

In some studies given to the quantification of data, in particular the sciences called social, fad and opinion hold sway, and investigators are known for the positions they take rather than for the facts they discover. And when social science turns into social action, ideological purity (whereby a man stands unshakable wherever he and his like-minded fellows stand) is valued above facts. Such purity resembles church orthodoxy so closely that it may well be theology's offspring. The purists inform me that God will be wroth if I, one small unit in the large human race, do not declare acceptance with mind and will of a series of their abstractions about him.

Such misuse of fact leads to calling things by name: scientific things like atoms, natural things like genera and species, divine things like theologies, and human things like behavior patterns. A considerable part of human learning amounts to little more than a pigeonholing of reality, very much in the manner of the stone-age people who sought control of things by knowing their secret names and by intoning the names under proper conditions and in suitable sequence. Trying to control reality by naming it—or by having a special vocabulary for describing it—is so unappealing to Lao Tzŭ, and using names to exalt self is so abhorrent, that his teaching may indeed be said to consist simply of not having names.

> Tao is always without name,
> Simple and small....
>
> When law and order arose,
> Names appeared.
> Aren't there enough already?
> Is it not time to stop?

When naming things nowadays, it is often possible to reinforce the names with numbers and thus to further the illusion of control over things. Or over people. Through intelligence tests, aptitude tests, and psychological tests, the *names* of the characteristics of individuals can be derived from the numerical positions they occupy on a master code of rank. These positions can then be used to determine the future of every human being as regards educational success, personal adjustment, and business and professional advancement. Thus are the superstitions of name and number ritualistically linked. But the consequence of such illusion is violence to fact and to the human beings subjected to it.

Crazy coding

Consider, for instance, the numerical nomenclature of the American Psychiatric Association, which has brought out during recent decades revised versions of its formidably titled "Diagnostic and Statistical Manual of Mental Disorders," the so-called DSM series, a code designed to rationalize the care of the irrationally ill. Essentially it is a ritualistic device that will complicate present treatment of psychiatric illnesses and confuse research into future treatments, but will do so in such a tidy numerical way as to suggest progress in mental health. The rationale of the code is to provide hundreds of numbered names and computerized numbers that are supposed to coincide with actual disease entities, and that can be used, first, as a basis for deciding treatment, second, as a method of research, and—when combined with a numerical scale of severity—third, hospitalization. Here the code enters into the semi-sacred area of hospital accreditation, government regulation, insurance payment, and malpractice protection, in which computer-derived data interface with computer-derived procedures, which can be handled by clerks. A code to satisfy the government and the insurers may be all very well (except for the patient caught in the middle of automaton-applied exclusions), but nobody knows whether there are any such things as specific disease entities in psychiatry. Many experienced practitioners believe that there is instead a spectrum of symptoms with one set of them fusing into the next without fixed boundaries. Patients are not this, that, or the other; rather they behave in this way, that way, or the other way. Factual symptoms rather than conceptual nomenclatures may well provide the most effective basis for treatment and research. In a conceptualized system, the patient gets lost and insight gets suppressed. The need is not to categorize, to judge, compare, contrast, and subject to theory. Rather the need is to be present repetitively and to be open to whatever is going on. Individual man, whether he is out of his mind or in it, is not much more understandable than the Tao from which he springs. Numerical nonsense of the DSM sort leads to treating the seriously ill briefly and ineffectively.

Useful stupidity

In short, the DSM code is a device for appearing knowledgeably in control of that which resists categorizing. Lao Tzŭ says "not to know but to be knowing is sickness," a condition he contrasts with "to know but to be unknowing." He attacks particularly the knowledgeability which denaturalizes and dehumanizes life. *Clever* is his word for it, and the word he sets in opposition is *stupid*. Stupidity clings to Tao; cleverness stirs up self.

> Why are the people hard to govern?
> Because they are too clever.
> Clever government is a curse,
> Non-clever government a blessing.
> To know these two things
> Is to follow the ancient pattern,
> And to know the ancient pattern
> Is original virtue.
> Original virtue is far-reaching and deep.
> It leads all things to return
> Back to the great harmony.

Nowhere has the Tao Teh Ching better demonstrated its social utility than in its critique of cleverness. It is the habit of governments to outfox themselves, and over the dynasties the simple teachings of Lao Tzŭ have helped sundry Chinese governments pause long enough to rescue themselves from at least a few of the consequences of overreaching themselves. Overreaching governments need nothing so much as Taoist stupidity, for they suffer from cleverness in advanced degrees, being led in some cases by men who read light fiction and watch television melodramas. Who but clever men could persuade themselves that supplying advanced weapons to almost all the powers in the Middle East would decrease the likelihood of the use of weapons there? Who but clever men could trade weapons for hostages with people who are against making trades? Who but they could invade a whole country to arrest one man? Who but they could react to a missile threat from one country with a plan to strike down the missiles of a second country in the belief that threats of war prevent war? And who, after winning a war, could try to lose it? Stupid men, hearing dogs bark, guess they might bite, for weak minds are not up to tricks of getting peace

out of bellicosity or of dealing secretly with open terrorism or of blaming a country like Iraq while mobilizing
openly against a second like Iran, which turns out not to
be nor to have been the actual enemy.

Perhaps no aspect of life in the United States has been
recently afflicted with a greater cleverness than the economic aspect, and certainly no topic has occasioned a
greater outpouring of political wisdom than inflation.
Many recent administrations, Republican and Democrat
alike, have been battling it, in the process manipulating
money and credit and eliminating the balances that used to
prevent special-interest groups from tipping the economic
scales to their benefit. The cleverness of the new balances
shows itself in an increasing tilt in favor of groups most
loudly demanding wealth, such as physicians, lawyers,
brokers, bankers, executives, and tin-horn entrepreneurs:
and against the unemployed and semi-employed poor,
who are thought to increase the cost of government, and
also against factory workers, whose wages are supposed to
increase inflation and discourage investment.

Foxy economics

The cleverness of such misalignment is suggested by
the many economic complications that have been ration-
alized away, such as decreasing industrial productivity
and decreasing attention to productivity, increasing industrial mergers and increasing interest in mergers. Ration-
alized also are the impacts of unbalanced fuel costs and
interest rates on costs and prices, of high-stake inter-
national and national loans, and of enormous and
uncontrollable military expenditures. Cleverly these are to
be paid for not by taxes but rather by high bank rates and
currency values—and then, abruptly, by collapsing the
values. American industrial productivity was sacrificed to
a clever economic theory of getting the benefit of
something by declining to pay for it. The clever man
remodels the economy to near-ruin. For him are the vast
economy-remolding conclusions. The stupid man, by con-

trast, puzzles over available facts, trusting that the facts themselves will eventually prompt the least dangerous course of action. Do not, Lao Tzŭ suggests, attempt to master the situation; keep to the facts. Let *them* lead:

> Many words exhaust sense.
> Keep to the empty center!

Tao's empty center is, among other things, the center of the multiform human personality, with its unfathomable ability to explore unconsciously and in detail entire fields of activity that the conscious mind overlooks, and to let courses of action emerge through rumination about facts rather than through conceptualization of them. Indeed, there is an entirely different way to look at reality from the conventional way that is held to be the only way.

Keep not to a guessing game

Yoked to a cogitated methodology, economics becomes possibly less reliable than a guessing game, which benefits at least from randomness. Pretensions to science, logic, and mathematics (now that the computer is upon us) make it possible to talk up notions that appear suicidal to anyone gifted with no more than average stupidity. Influential economists are quite able to explain such matters as the revolutionary change-over of an economy long based on low-cost fuel and low-cost money to one newly based on high costs: costs that almost overwhelmed the automobile, construction, metallurgical, and manufacturing industries, along with savings and commercial banks—and, when prices eventually dropped, the fuel industries themselves.

Meanwhile government experts saluted the new service economy, even though it appeared to be based on every person living off every other person through intangible interchange financed by skyrocketing debt: the production of tangibles having been laid aside as out of keeping with lower wages and quicker profits. These ins and outs, the stupid man suspects, are likely to end sooner or later in some sort of economic upheaval, but the clever man has developed a mental grid through which he strains what is going on and by means of which he rejects what does not fit the grid. How else could he support the adage, which rose to popularity in the 1920s, that the cause of inflation is simply and exclusively the cost of government? Or the new belief that huge military budgets can be met not through taxes or savings but through the sale of high-interest bonds to foreigners? Myth is often the vehicle by which rational men account for reality.

Monetary Olympians

Only a few decades ago, there were said to be not more than a dozen individuals in the country able to discuss such topics as the cost of money, the flow of money, and what might be called the equation of money. When these individuals talked, most bankers and economists took leave. The topics were held to be too complicated for general discussion. Indeed, the equation of money is influenced literally by everything that happens throughout the world, including what is said to be a part of economics and a very great deal of what is said to be no part of it. Included, in particular, are psychological factors dismissed conventionally as indeterminable.

Money can be said to move in the manner of a mobile of gigantic complexity, all of whose innumerable units can be put into varying and unexpected rates of motion by the simple touching of one very small and distant unit. Money experts used to wait months and even years, watching not for the right answers to give but for the right questions to ask, playing in this way the wait-and-see game of Taoist stupidity. Nowadays, however, clever bureaucrats and economists have taken courage from the simplified models their computers so readily turn out. They know about money; they know about inflation (even after the onset of deflation in the early 1980s many still thought a little bit of deflation a good thing); they know all about interest rates, trade balances, currency levels, productivity, and the many factors that look countable, but are not necessarily the factors that should be counted.

The clever answer to the productivity problems was to divert money into investment. But the problems date not from some supposititious time when investment capital started to dry up, but rather from an actual time some forty years ago when investors began to develop an appetite not for productivity but for quick profits from mergers, acquisitions, conglomerates, and takeovers: in preference to the slower profits that accrue from funding higher output and lower prices, the true essence of productivity. Forgotten was the phenomenal outpouring of goods during the second World War and the immediate post-war period, along with the dedication to public service developed during those times. Emphasis on productivity (in the broader sense of output rather than in the narrower sense of labor costs) was then carried to the degree of preoccupation with it; it was thought to be the only way of carrying so enormously wasteful an operation as war.

Economic wastelands

Now there seems to be difficulty carrying the more limited but still enormous wastes of peace: e.g., the operations of the unneeded-goods sector of the economy, the useless services sector, and the now-huge sector of unnecessary services, ranging from poor-food outlets to fancy resorts, entities that are now bigger than the productive plant on which they feed. Then there are other drains on productivity: the theft and chicanery sector of the economy together with those sectors that try to put down theft and chicanery through legal, penal, and military systems. The portion of the country's economic effort used up in attempts to curb wrongdoing is alone enormous and, like other drone operations, it tends to imbalance the economy. But such matters are now beyond critical discussions in public.

Many economic problems are beyond discussion. At any given time in any given culture, people probably do

71

not really know what their basic economic problems are. Otherwise they would have been easier to solve. Feudal Japan, for example, suffered recurrent problems of price levels and tax rates. It is now evident, as Sir George Sansom was among the first to point out, that these problems arose from a serious imbalance in the number of idle aristocrats and the number of farmers who grew rice to feed them. But, despite widespread awareness of the problems, no one at the time was aware of the imbalance (hierarchic matters being *sui generis*) even though a new social class was coming into existence partially as a result of it. Probably the American economy has problems of comparable import of which people today are similarly unaware, possibly as concerns economic effort lost in a wide variety of drone operations or wasted in supporting shibboleths about competition.

Meanwhile there is the other Way, a way in which not ignorance but awareness is the consequence of being unknowing as to myth and open-minded as to fact:

> The lesson of nothing-speaking,
> The use of nothing-doing:
> Rare attainments beneath Heaven!

For when experts fail, only nothing-knowing can succeed. A passive waiting for something to happen is transformed into an active force by simple awareness of the Way by which things happen whenever people are willing to let them. It is a way of getting outward results by inward stillness and sureness. It is a way of insight, a way of bearing the confusions of life until answers to problems work their way to the surface of consciousness. The contrary way of outward knowledge, of identifying the causes of problems, of assembling pertinent facts, and of drawing logical conclusions, appears to be a way out of confusion. But it is no way out at all, since what is causal, what is pertinent, and what is logical are questions too intricate for conscious human untangling, whenever, at least, there is

72

more involved than simple objects and numbers. Why not welcome confusion? Why let it lead to frustration and then solidify into neurosis? Confusion is a natural state of being from which, whenever it is comfortably borne, meaning emerges.

Cleverness lacks meaning; it provides little more than egocentric thrill. When meaning is absent, social dissolution starts to occur, and the ordinary activities of life become as if tinged with death. Yet when cleverness disappears, Tao remains. Tao is found whenever sought.

5.
Nothing-
Wanting

The Tao Teh Ching is purposefully non-sequential, carefully repetitive, and intentionally non-conclusive. It is not trying to get anywhere since it is on the way there already. One saying follows another, often repeating the other, without following the precedences of logic. The book itself is an insight composed of many separate insights of style and form and flavor that, to reemphasize, are not separate entities but all of one piece. In like manner, Gandhi emphasizes that the three aspects of Truth, non-violence, and simplicity have but one aspect. In the book of Tao, wholeness is the essence of nothing-doing, of nothing-knowing, and of nothing-wanting.

> Keep to simplicity,
> Grasp the primal,
> Reduce the self,
> And curb desire.

What people want depends, obviously, on how they look at life, all of it, everything around them. Lao Tzŭ takes this truism much further out, maintaining that not wanting anything is the only useful way of wanting: wanting, that is, the simple, the unclouded, the selfless. Wanting things for oneself is of a piece with doing things violently and cogitating things cleverly. Quaker George Fox regularly equated coveting with fighting.

Lao Tzŭ's word for simplicity, nothing-wanting, is neither an action nor a non-action but a state of being. And while he counsels against possession of people and things, he by no means counsels retreat from life and from other people in the guise of non-involvement and non-attachment. He decries attachment to self and involvement with self, warning against anything that separates from the primal, anything that enlarges the self, anything that encourages the covetous. The counsel of nothing-doing leads to simplicity anyone wanting—at least half-heartedly—to get there.

> No calamity is greater
> Than not knowing what is enough,
> No fault worse than wanting too much.
> Whoever knows what is enough has enough.

How does a person know what is enough? Certainly he does not discover such a limit by himself, even though it can only be found within him. Something outside makes the inward discovery for him, and that outside something may be custom or may be Tao: Tao as Tao or as whatever word be used to indicate the source of meaningfulness in life. In times when custom is sloughing off meaningfulness like old garments turned rotten, it is not until a person turns to the Way that he can simplify his existence. To pauperize existence consciously is more often than not to complicate it. And it may well be that he turns to Tao only because his life is so complex that it has become unbearably flat. Bafflement—not confusion, which is a normal part of life—oppresses him, overwhelms him, crowds in around him, topples him, and threatens to pull him under, crush him, and bury him.

Lost purpose and forgotten meaning

Certainly the complexities of contemporary life are the inseparable consequence of lost purpose and forgotten meaning. Many people act as if they wanted as a matter of choice to be forlorn, frustrated, and forsaken, as if they wished to live surrounded by an atmosphere of distress. In literature there is a marked absence of purpose outside self; there is not even a commonly accepted body of learning, not even enough for literary allusions. Other arts reflect rootlessness, and painting at times rejects the ways of nature to fragment space and the beings occupying it. It seems to make little difference whether a person goes to church or lies abed of Sundays; he suffers from an absence of significance, and his centeredness on self does not rescue him from a paralysis of purpose. He feels the dull ache of aloneness, the swirling vacuity of frustration; and some sense tells him that he is beset with deadness.

The misery of this deadness is too suffocating to bear. Besides, it is productive of exhausting tensions and angers when one miserable person confronts another person equally miserable. Exhaustion swells emptiness into an agitated emptiness; the imperative to find a way out of this deadness becomes desperate, and unless a true Way is found, it is easy to end up in one of a number of dead-end streets. Four of these dead-ends, which are simply escapes so unsuccessful that they seem to have been predesigned for failure, come at once to mind.

One escape is to cast off restraints on behavior in the conviction that, Tao having been overthrown, anything is permissible. Whether the anything is sex, success, or crime, it is made the occasion for sudden upsurges of excitement that reflect the hope that all life will be one long binge. Since life is patently no such picnic, this escape sooner or later closes up, usually sooner than later: it cannot survive the interruptions of daily existence or the interference of falling sick, getting old, and running short of money.

The second escape, probably the principal escape in the Bronze Age and not an infrequent one in an age of computers, is concentration on personal possessions and on the inward covetousness that spurs acquisition of them, leading to such common acts as addictive buying and compulsive self-decoration. This escape is a brittle one. "Do not," advises Lao Tzŭ, "shine like jade or tinkle like stone chimes."

Hold onto fullness?
It is better to stop.
Handle sharp edges?
They can't long be kept.
When gold and jade fill a house,
No one can protect it.
Pride in wealth and fame
Breeds its own collapse.

In an age when there is little gold, not much jade, and no stone chimes, Lao Tzŭ's advice is often extended to material objects in general. His advice actually pertains not to objects but to preoccupation with them. Some earnest people believe that having anything more than blue jeans, brown rice, new wine, and no heat is an obstacle to Truth so great that a search for it cannot even be started. This convenient excuse is sometimes offered by people of higher education and lower income, whose possessions are typically not material but personal, consisting of their offspring, their spouses, their books, and the more mentionable of their friends. But they wear the people and the books around them with as much éclat as the rich wear fur coats and rare-metal watches. This sort of escape begins to fail when decorations go away or else begin to talk back.

A third escape is a falling back willy-nilly on precisely those conventionalities in which one was brought up, perhaps under the illusion that whatever produced such a person as oneself must be life's true guide, a guide to how children should be raised or the house cleaned or the thermostat set. The attractiveness of this escape is usually blocked by hurt feelings and hard feelings when people nearby decline to follow the true guide, even when particularly requested to follow it. Moreover, the request tends to exacerbate hard feelings toward the very guides who begot the request. Hatred chains many people to their parents more tightly than does affection.

Compulsive escape

A fourth escape is by way of compulsions, including obvious addiction to alcohol and drugs, together with more subtle habituation to selected neuroses and to hidden fascinations and intoxications of a subclinical sort. The insidiousness of such escapes lies in the illusion that compulsive dedication to particular things, rituals, and emotions will clarify life out of confusion, simplify it out of complexity, and lift it out of inertness. A vain hope. People clamoring to be overawed by compulsions are usually overwhelmed by the inward racket stirred by the very compulsions themselves, and the racket does not go away until an end is made of wanting anything. Wistful hopes for simplicity cannot arrest the increasing complications of the addicted life.

Specific addiction to alcohol and drugs is recognized almost universally as a compulsive effort at escape, even though it often seems uncertain what is being escaped from. The victims of addiction themselves feel certain that they are escaping from something specific in the form of outside pressures and injustices, but the more they escape, the more uncertain they are whether they are getting away from anything. Frustration ensues, and this mood can be changed only through more alcohol and drugs until all mood is obliterated in the vacancies of druggedness and drunkenness and eventually of death. Of such addiction, the words of the Tao Teh Ching have a pertinence so obvious as to be amusing:

> Knowing what is enough avoids disgrace;
> Knowing when to stop secures from peril.

It is, of course, precisely the nature of compulsion to render addicts unable to know what or when to stop. They are powerless to get over their disease through any operations of their own minds and intelligences; the disease, indeed, has been called "self-will run riot." It is possible to recover from it by abandoning self-will along with the urge to know the why of addiction, a process undertaken in the mutual-aid groups of Alcoholics Anonymous whenever the addict becomes willing to surrender his will to that of a Power greater than himself, personified in the group. Will is traded in on recovery.

The compulsive character of these neuroses is evident to persons suffering from them, and these complaints have been successfully treated as if they were compulsions by encouraging surrender of self-will. But such treatment is new and relatively unknown. Only selected fears and cravings are usually named compulsive by psychotherapists. Treatment of the common conditions of fear, rage, depression, and guilt, together with the syndrome wherein all these conditions chase each other around in a circle, is thought to require an understanding of the illness and an analysis of its causes: in short, cerebral control of recovery from a disease characterized by cerebral efforts to control life, very often by compulsive devices. Analysis may indeed be part of the disease. Relatively few patients appear to be lifted out of affliction by these devices, and in most cases the benefits of psychotherapy are palliative, resulting in large part perhaps from personal confirmation by a concerned therapist or group. The mental health industry is as conventional as most other industries, and nothing-wanting is not part of the business.

Things good in themselves

When compulsion operates on subclinical levels, it is seldom recognized as compulsion or as anything anyone ought to get over, for it is seen as nothing more than the inordinate pursuit of things commonly considered good in themselves, such as work, housecleaning, church-going, book-reading, book-writing, picture-making, education, concert-attending, and gift-giving. There is actually little difference between chasing these things inherently good and seeking more dubious escapes in the thrills, violences, and artificial emotionalism of television and the movies. When the pursuit of anything at all, whether good or bad, involves dependency on it, that thing plays the same role as do more obvious compulsions. Such things are pursued relentlessly because they hide reality and indulge self.

Compulsion, indeed, is inwardly more destructive than the objects pursued. The practices of churches can be as destructive as the tantrums of households. Immersion in hard work can be as overwhelming as immersion in drink. Reading literature can be as heady as shooting drugs. Prayer can be turned into self-worship. Only the Way itself allows of inordinate pursuit; the inordinate pursuit of anything else ends in destruction, even the pursuit of social good. When it becomes a compulsion, it is as destructive (to society as well as to self) to chase after it as it is to chase after status and riches and fame; and it is doubly destructive to be clever about it.

> When Tao is cast aside,
> Duty and humanity abide.
> When prudence and wit appear,
> Great hypocrites are here.

The illusory pursuit of compulsions or possessions is typically accompanied by ritual: that is, by a ceremonious repetitiveness that aims to give irrationalities and egocentricities the appearance, if not of righteousness, at least of style. It occupies a place far down on a descending scale of aberrations. ("When morality is lost, there is ceremony. Now ceremony is the shell of loyalty and distrust and the beginning of confusion.") Even farther down the list is divination and the sundry forms of ancient and contemporary superstition.

> As to foreknowledge,
> It is a blossomy path
> And the beginning of folly.

The notion that nature can be magically manipulated to further personal interests is foreign to the Tao Teh Ching.

In view of the association of later Taoism with magic and foretelling and the occult in general, it is well to emphasize that the Taoism of Lao Tzŭ is not less iconoclastic than other prophetic faiths. The I Ching, a work now popular among Westerners, reflects a mixture of wisdom and divination characteristic of the Chou dynasty during which Lao Tzŭ lived, but its conventionality and superstition are not Tao but what Tao is against.

What of the religion of personal health, perhaps the only ancient form of faith still thriving in Europe and America? A system of belief replete with rules of diets, lists of proper exercises, precepts about good potions and bad potions, and prohibitions of self-harming activities, it is shunned by Lao Tzŭ with the same vigor he shuns other forms of preoccupation with self. The Tao Teh Ching, in a comment about interfering with creation, describes as injurious a practice that much later became a popular system of self-fitness and self-spirituality:

> It is ominous
> To improve on life,
> Violent to
> Control breathing by the mind:
> Things overgrown fall into decay.
> This is not-Tao,
> And what is not-Tao soon ends.

Conversely, what is Tao never ends. Once the something-doing, something-knowing, and something-wanting compulsions of self-will are cast aside, the Way opens. But that is the next chapter.

6.
The Success
of Failure

There is a general misapprehension that the Way of the prophets—of Isaiah, of Lao Tzŭ, of Gautama, of Jesus—is a very exalted way that can be followed only by very remarkable people, and that it requires a giving up of the normal activities and emotions of mankind and a rising to heights of spirit which few human beings are capable of achieving. In the light of the teachings of the prophets, concerned with ordinary people in ordinary walks of life, this misapprehension is nonsense. It is convention's effort to keep people under the dead hand of the past, to preserve at all costs the sway of violence and oppression and acquisitiveness and compulsion, and to prevent people from grasping the fact that they have only to become sick of their sickness to be set free from it. It is as if a man, seated on a stove that becomes hot, were to be informed that heroic fortitude would be required for him to get off, when all he needs is an ordinary response to discomfort. Actually, it takes great and endless fortitude to persist in old pains of fearfulness, aloneness, depression, and rage: all of them pregnant of hurt.

Give up!

It is no different when people are sitting on their sick selves, for the emotional pain of chasing success and having unsuccessful run-ins with other people, of grasping knowledge and ending up possessed by possessions and compelled by compulsions: such pain can be as intense as any discomfort human beings can suffer. To get rid of the pain, nothing more is needed than a willingness to admit failure and to give up and get away. It then becomes possible to accept life rather than battle it, to simplify it rather than complicate it, to be open to it rather than understand it. The sententious notion that man must know himself is put aside, and an inward sense suggests that the self our society teaches people to seek is the self that it is impossible for a person to know. True knowledge is social rather than solitary, and the true self is not so much knowing as knowable. A person who looks into a mirror hardly recognizes himself and sometimes cowers before the strange image confronting him, but his friends know him unerringly at fifty paces and judge correctly the state of his mind from the tilt of his back. Such awareness proceeds from the uncluttered emptiness of Tao, an emptiness that revives.

> Tao is empty! Use it
> And it isn't used up.
> Deep! It seems like
> The forebear of
> The ten thousand things.
> It blunts edges,
> Unties tangles,
> Harmonizes lights,
> Unites all dusts.
>
> Submerged and existent!
> I don't know whose child it is.
> It looks to be the source.

Tao liberates

For once success has finally failed, Tao liberates; Truth liberates; the God of the prophets liberates. Men and women come to realize that inward comfort and meaning are not to be found in what people try to make happen, but only in what actually happens. People then find more than comfort and meaning. They find joy and awe, sometimes suffering, but always awe and through the awe, joy. Similarly, people come to recognize that they can find no com-

83

fort and meaning in self, that such are to be found only in the Way. And here they find the reward of failure: the stillness that is simplicity.

> All men have plenty;
> I alone am a loser,
> A fool at heart indeed!
> And stupid stupid!
> The world's people are bright bright;
> I alone am dull dull!
> The world's people are smart smart;
> I alone am low low,
> Bland as the sea,
> Aimless as the wind.

> All men have their uses;
> I alone am stubborn and uncouth.
> But I differ most from the others
> In prizing food drawn from my Mother.

But such personal advantage can be found only socially. The Way can be followed—and prophetic faith in general can be experienced—only to the degree that an individual has life and being in a group. In the Bronze Age, there were at least remnants of a Golden Age to be observed in the lives of the common people and the barbarians to whom Lao Tzŭ felt himself compelled to flee. In an age in which the remnants are hidden underneath a self-willfulness that threatens life's continuance, there are yet many inner sources of strength, the scriptures of the Way for example. But the way of learning the Way is by looking at it as a group of persons and also walking along it as a group of persons.

The Way is social also in the manner by which individuals can witness against violence and oppression. A group of people, inwardly concerned for peace rather than willful for outward success, can show the depth of their concern by taking trouble and suffering upon themselves (not, note well, by imposing trouble and suffering on others), and can in this way operate in the realm of spiritual reality, appealing to the deeper levels of being that people usually forget they possess. Thus did the followers of Gandhi appeal in their various campaigns against untouchability in India, showing their concern by standing for very long periods of time in an attitude of prayer. So did the followers of Martin Luther King Jr., in their protracted vigils and marches.

These groups in effect renounced success; they came to realize that concerns of peace and freedom can prevail only when other people, in particular those who stand in an opponent relationship, are inwardly lifted out of themselves. The getting of publicity, the calling of epithets, the brandishing of signs, and the enacting of skits and the burning of dummies produce no inward lifting, which is the result not of cleverness but of example. To trust the Way that directs to peace is to trust its natural operations in the hearts of human beings once it is clearly shown to them. The Way the universe is constructed is the Way along which human beings sooner or later will come to walk. It is a Way not of justice or any other retribution, not of drama or any other racket. It is a Way of simple and affectionate concern.

> The sage has no fixed heart.
> He finds his heart
> In the hundred families' hearts.
> He is good to the good;
> He is also good to the not-good.
> For virtue is good.
> He is faithful to the faithful;
> He is also faithful to the unfaithful,
> For virtue is faithful.

The path not the end of the path

The Way, clearly, is the Way of the Kingdom of Heaven, but the kingdom is not simply at the end of the path; it

85

is also the path itself. Truth may someday triumph totally, but the contribution of the billions of men and women and children to that triumph are small daily triumphs, and it is to these that Truth impels them. In history as in personal life, a very little bit of Tao goes a long way, and a turning to Tao that is hesitating and incomplete can mean life itself for a sick world and for sick people trying to keep alive in it. It can make all things new, and bring people to a new stillness and a new simplicity, so that they come to resemble the ancient masters:

> Tao's ancient masters were
> Inwardly subtle and darkly perceptive.
> Their depth was beyond understanding.
>
> Because they were beyond understanding,
> They can be described only by appearance:
> Hesitant as if wading a river in winter,
> Reluctant as if fearing a neighbor,
> Reserved as if acting as guest,
> Effacing like ice starting to melt,
> Simple like uncarved wood,
> Open like a valley,
> Confused like muddy water.
>
> Who else could clear muddy water
> By quieting it?
> Who else could move clear water
> By bringing it to life?

For the changes in human affairs that take place in time result less from conscious planning and projecting, more from the inward yearnings of people's hearts, of all the people's hearts. Rulers can express themselves outwardly about the shape of the future, about how it should be arranged, whether it is to be peaceful or warlike, dynamic or static, but the future will take shape in terms not of how they express themselves, but of how all the people live. In the light of the Way, problems arrange themselves if they are let to do so. Lao Tzŭ advises, "Rule a big country as you would cook a small fish," a useful counsel of nothing-doing in a society that tends in its kitchens to desiccate meat and in its assembly halls to overcook life. There is only one Way to cook and one Way to live.

> From of old
> Its name has not ceased,
> For it has watched all beginnings.
> How can all beginnings be watched?
> Inward Light!

Part II. The Tao/Virtue Classic
Introduction

The Tao Teh Ching is addressed to all aspects of man, including that part which is as submerged as the bulk of an iceberg and measurably more immeasurable. For several millenia Asia's most read book, it has been often translated, but typically it has been addressed to the visible part of Western man that passes for conscious reason. The habit of translators is to make the original understandable, to explain it. But how shall one attempt to explain a book that deals with the inexplicable? Lao Tzŭ is to be read with the eyes and felt in the belly with minimal interference from the head. He is to be dipped into, lived with, perused again and again, but without regularity or purpose. His book is an invitation to insight, not cogitation.

It is in the original stark, vivid, simple. To transfer its terseness and impact from ancient Chinese characters to modern English phonetics is to tamper with it, although attempt has been made to reduce drastically the translated words and to arrange them on the page in a way that transmits a feeling for the original. Simply to print the Tao Teh Ching in a phoneticized language is to do considerable violence to its original eloquence, which depends on look more than on sound.

When translation imposes upon their inherent limitations superfluous explanation to distant foreigners of what the original author had in his thoughts, the result is not clarity but diffuseness, and the author is lost.

Exactness

The present rendering of Lao Tzŭ attempts to carry on a tradition of translation to which Dr. John C.H.Wu and Dr.

Lin Yutang belong. The two men understood the original because they not only studied but also experienced it. Dr. Wu's translation is a work not only of long study but also of profound meditation and broad exposure to life, for he served as jurist, ambassador, professor of law, and member of the World Court at the Hague. Dr. Lin's translation is a key part of his extensive efforts to introduce Chinese thought to a Western public, including the new thought that emerged from the Chinese literary renaissance. Some experts, including the noted Arthur Waley, dismiss such translations as scriptural as opposed to scholarly, but the Waley translation is itself diffuse, wordy, and, in its attempts at conceptual understanding, remarkably inexact. The present translation seeks to build on a more literal and more Taoist tradition.

Its aim, consequently, is to try to preserve the force, rhythm, repetitions, and parallelisms of the original, and even attempt a pun or two and an occasional rhyme. It declines to defer to the conceptual habits of Westerners by rendering such terms of Chinese concreteness as *the ten thousand things, the hundred families,* and *beneath heaven* into such abstractions as *all things, the people,* and *the world.* It may be said that the finite is bigger than the infinite; somebody is more real than everybody; and the bounded is more extensive than the unbounded. When, however, consistency would upset style, the shorter terms are used. The manner in which the Way is presented is also the Way.

Sight *vs.* sound

While the translation seeks to be as exact in word as possible, exactness is impossible with a work of the spirit composed in the early morning of man's history, and some exactness of translation is possible only by recognizing that full exactness is not to be had. Generally, the translation tries to tamper least with the terseness and impact of the original. It makes no effort to explain the inexplicable, and it also avoids trying to make clear what is not clear.

The Tao Teh Ching is not to be explained and understood; it is to be sensed, seen, smelled, tasted even, and mindlessly and mindfully assimilated.

The absence of headings for chapters or other divisions in the original work makes for troubles in the use of the Tao Teh Ching in translated form. There is no narrative, no progression of logic, and not even connected argument in terms of which individual sentences, paragraphs, and chapters can be located. Persons to whom the Chinese language is native seem to have less difficulty locating passages than do Westerners, largely, I suspect, because early and long acquaintance with ideographic characters, which occupy space rather than define sound, trains memory of a visual sort to remarkable acuteness and makes it possible to locate quickly passages in most well-read texts. But this memory is seldom available to Westerners. Therefore titles, which depend more on sound than on space, have been foisted upon all the eighty-one chapters of the Tao Teh Ching. (These titles are included in the index.) In the commentary section of the book, notes and comments have been appended to the various chapters in the thought that it is better to talk about the text than to try to make the text talk about itself. The aim of these comments is to assist introduction to Lao Tzŭ through short signpost statements, comments on particular problems of the text, and brief quotations principally from Isaiah, Jesus, and the prophetic teachers of Quakerism and Hasidism. The notes indicate how the present translation differs from others whenever differences are marked.

It is not the notes, however, but the text that is to be read again and again—and without conscious attempt at comprehension. Scripture must dawn on the readers of it. This commentary on Lao Tzŭ is introductory: it is designed to render itself superfluous so that the reader can bring to mind not it but that remarkable work, the text. The translation of it is therefore printed without comment or title directly following the commentary. (First lines are included in the index.) Perhaps it would be better to comment not at all. The true scriptures, it is said, are those which appear as blank pages, for words fail when they are applied to that which is beyond words. But once the in-evitability of such failure is recognized, it is possible to let untruth instruct in Truth, in the same way that noise instructs in silence. After all, Lao Tzŭ says that he who speaks does not know and he who knows does not speak, but he sets down a speaking for our instruction. Perhaps his book, which has spoken to so many millions of per-sons over the millenia, can be described as a joyful noise unto Tao that leads to true stillness.

Manual for wholeness

The noise and stillness are pertinent to men and women everywhere, but it is important to remember that Lao Tzŭ addressed himself to rulers and their scholar-assistants, partly for the very simple reason that they were the only persons in his times who knew how to read. The book sometimes sounds like a manual of topsy-turvy govern-ment, and indeed it has been used as such during sundry short stretches of Chinese history. It has been useful during longer stretches as a manual for non-government, but it is also a manual for marriage, for business, for education, and for any situation in which persons meet persons and in which persons meet nature. It is a guide on how persons can remain whole in times of confusion. And it is constantly a book of hints on how to meet Tao.

The sixth century B.C. is the traditional date of Lao Tzŭ, but tradition has been widely attacked by practitioners of both the higher and lower criticisms. Possibly no-criticism (like no-knowledge) is best. Many years ago, Dr. Hu Shih wrote a monograph entitled "A Criticism of Some Recent Methods Used in Dating Lao Tzŭ," (*Harvard Journal of Asiatic Studies*, 2, December 1937), a study of the difficulties and logical improbabili-ties of dating early writings by comparing them with other writings whose dates are not firm or with cultural fac-tors—customs, style, ideas, vocabularies, grammatical constructions—which occurred over broad periods of time. Dr. Hu concluded, as did Professor Martin Buber for the Jewish scriptures, that tradition provides a more dependable method of literary transmission than many scholars imagine.

However important dates are to scholars, they are of less importance to general readers, concerned with what is said rather than when it is said. In terms of Lao Tzǔ's writings about knowing-nothing, it is unimportant when he lived or whether he lived. But it is significant that the recent Mawangtui manuscripts can be dated at 168 B.C., not only from internal evidence but also from a memorandum enclosed in the grave in which they were found. The differences between these manuscripts and the Wang Pi text are minor enough to suggest the cautious transmission and substantial degree of accuracy of many early Chinese writings. Most changes in the texts of the Tao Teh Ching may well have been made before the Han dynasty, which began in 206 B.C. (See Appendix, p. 237.)

The changes that have taken place since include the division of the book into short units known as chapters. In the second century B.C., the only division was between upper and lower parts, one starting off with Tao and the other with Teh. The later chapter divisions were entirely a matter of convention, and the still later division into paragraphs has been and continues to be according to the whim of commentators and translators.

The question of what parts of the Tao Teh Ching were written when, changed how, rewritten in what way, and finally put together for what reason in the earlier manuscripts: these are continuing challenges for the scholars. To suffering and seeking human beings, the challenge is the book itself. The Tao Teh Ching has been since its inception a living, growing thing, and thanks should be given to the many hands that have reached out to it, not least to the Confucian scholars who edited it but kept it alive in times of their own orthodoxy.

The Tao/Virtue Classic
Commentary

1.

Tao Can't Be Taoed

If Tao can be Taoed, it's not Tao.
If its name can be named, it's not its name.
Has no name: precedes heaven and earth;
Has a name: mother of the ten thousand things.

For it is
Always dispassionate:
See its inwardness;
Always passionate:
See its outwardness.

The names are different
But the source the same.
Call the sameness mystery:
Mystery of mystery, the door to inwardness.

Beyond words is Tao! The opening passage of the Tao Teh Ching has the vigor of the first sentence of the book of John: "In the beginning was the word, and the word was with God, and the Word was God." But here majesty is admixed with paradox and humor. The impact of the first line is multiplied by an additional meaning that hinges on a divine pun, "If the path can be followed, it's not the path," and also by a derivative meaning with the sense of "If God gods it, he's not God."

In the original, the word *constant* modifies the second use of *Tao* in line one (and in line two the second use of *name*). It has been omitted in translation because the impact of the rhythm of the sentence, as significant as the sense, is upset, and because the Western reader is not likely to imagine Tao as anything but an absolute. In Chinese, *Tao* also means *Path* or *path*, since ancient times its primary meaning, and the modifier *constant* is needed to differentiate the extraordinary from the ordinary. (Except, of course, that the ordinary is more extraordinary than the extraordinary.)

The phrase *ten thousand things* is usually rendered as *all things*, and the phrase *heaven and earth* as *the universe*. Chinese ideographs encourage concreteness.

2.

Takes No Credit

When all beneath heaven
Know beauty as beauty,
There is not beauty.
When all know good as good,
There is not good.

For what is and what is not beget each other;
Difficult and easy complete each other;
Long and short show each other;
High and low place each other;
Noise and sound harmonize each other;
Before and behind follow each other.

Therefore the sage
Manages without doing,
Teaches without talking.
He does not shun
The ten thousand things:
Rears them without owning them,
Works for them without claiming them,
Accomplishes but takes no credit.

Because he does not take credit,
It cannot be taken from him.

Beyond opposites is Tao! Often assumed to be a statement of the relativity of values, this chapter is actually a song of praise to the beyond-everything wholeness of Tao. Anything less than Tao is so immensely less that the differences between anything less and its opposite are of little significance. A turning *from* ordinary differentiation enables the sage to find closeness to Tao and enables him to accomplish but take no credit.

An eighteenth-century Hasidic teacher, Yehiel Michal of Zlotchov, noted that "if there were no evil, there would be no good, for good is the counterpart of evil. Everlasting delight is no delight.... [T]he fact that evil confronts good gives man the possibility of victory." [*Tales*, p. 144]

Beneath heaven is typically translated as *the world*, a place of many meanings and a term of no location. *Therefore*, in classical Chinese, means simply that there is a link between what goes before and what comes after, but not that there is a causal or even sequential relationship. The logic of the Chinese language includes an indeterminism of intermingling happenings, which are not strictly causal. In this translation, *for*, *hence*, *now*, *so*, *also*, and *thus* often substitute for *therefore*.

3.

Takes No Credit

If you don't exalt the worthy:
People then will not compete.
If you don't prize rare goods:
People then will not steal.
If you don't show what is covetable:
The people's hearts won't be upset.

Thus, when the sage rules,
He empties hearts

And fills bellies,
Weakens ambitions
And strengthens bones.

He leads the people
To not-know and not-want,
And the cunning ones
To dare not do.
By doing nothing-doing,
Everything gets done.

Setting an example of contention is a typical occasion for contention. Quaker John Woolman, writer of journals and worker against slavery, wrote in the eighteenth century about "ways of living attended with unnecessary labor … which draw forth the minds of many people to seek after outward power and to strive for riches, which frequently introduce oppression and bring forth wars." [Considerations of Pure Wisdom and Human Policy, 1768]

Isaac Penington, a seventeenth-century devotionalist, wrote about the value of not knowing: "Be still and wait for light and strength and desire not to know or comprehend.…" [*Letters*, John Barclay edition, p. 173]

When the sage *empties hearts and fills bellies*, he meets needs but shuns covetousness. He also encourages humility. In Chinese, *empty-hearted* means *humble*. As for the full belly, eating at a shared table has long been held as worshipful among Chinese as it has among Jews.

The famous adage of *wei wu wei*, here translated as *doing nothing-doing*, is the positive form of *wu wei*, literally *not-do*, and thus signifies *do not-do*. Its full meaning, to be grasped only in context, embraces not alone the wisdom of non-interference, but in addition the forcefulness of taking action in the realm of the inward: *i.e.,* the realm of nothingness that is accessible only through humility. In this realm, humility is positive and passivity is dynamic; purposive action is static. Nothing-doing gets things done; something-doing does not.

4.

Use Emptiness!

Tao is empty! Use it
And it isn't used up.
Deep! It seems like
The forebear of
The ten thousand things.
It blunts edges,
Unties tangles,
Harmonizes lights,
Unites all dusts.

Submerged and existent!
I don't know whose child it is.
It looks to be the source.

Apparently different in manner and meaning from Lao Tzŭ's hymn of praise is the hymn of praise of the later Isaiah, but the common sense of awe is nearly identical.

Who ever measured the waters in the hollow
 of his hand
or ruled the skies off with a span,
or held the dust of earth inside a measure,
or weighed the mountains in a pair of scales,
 the hills within a balance?
Who ever moved the mind of the Eternal,
or gave him lessons and advice?
Who ever was called in to give him counsel?
Who ever taught him how to act, or showed him
 what to do?

[Isaiah 40:12-14, Moffatt translation] Differences in the outer clothing of words are swallowed up in wonder at the pervasiveness of the Undefined, the Unknown, the Ever-present, whether the nameless and inexplicable YHVH or the nameless and inexplicable Tao. John Woolman says:

"There is a principle which is pure, placed in the human mind, which in different places and ages hath had different names. It is, however, pure and proceeds from God. It is deep and inward, confined to no forms of religion nor excluded from any where the heart stands in perfect sincerity. In whomsoever this takes root and grows, of what nation soever, they become brothers in the best sense of the expression. Using ourselves to take ways which appear most easy to us, when inconsistent with that purity which is without beginning, we thereby set up a government of our own and deny obedience to him whose service is true liberty." [Considerations On Keeping Negroes, Part Second, 1762]

5.

Straw Dogs

Heaven-and-earth is not humane:
It treats the ten thousand things
Like straw dogs.
The sage is not humane:
He treats the hundred families
Like straw dogs.

Heaven-and-earth and all between
Is like a bellows:
Empty but never used up.
The more it moves,
The more comes out of it.

Many words exhaust sense.
Keep to the empty center!

How life-giving is the impartiality of heaven and earth! Treating all the people *like straw dogs* (that is, like

98

things of nominal worth that are burned in funeral rites) means treating all of them exactly alike, without regard for their goodness or badness. The sage thus acts in consonance with the One who causes his rain to fall on the just and the unjust.

Tao is sometimes conceptualized into a force, remote from human affairs, that acts as impersonally as the law of gravity, and this technicality is true of Tao as it is true of the God of the prophets, but it is by no means the whole Truth. The whole Truth is Tao itself, no non-entity but a Mother, personal and impersonal, who is beyond impersonality and personality, whose breasts the sage sucks (see Chapter 20), and whose reality is known to human beings through the sensation of inward warmth and light that follows dethronement of self-will. Tao is not less immanent than it is transcendent, but concepts cannot reveal Tao. They hide it.

The hundred families is usually translated as *the people*. Chinese family names are numbered in the countable hundreds. Chapter 11 persuades this translator to add the word *empty* to the last line to indicate early Taoist distrust of a middle course.

6.

Use It and It Won't Wear Out

The spirit of low places does not die.
Call its mysteriousness feminine.
The gate of this mysteriousness
Is the source of heaven-and-earth.
Unceasingly, unceasingly it seems to persist.
Use it and it won't wear out.

Only from low places is it possible to look upon heaven-and-earth. From high places, the temptation is to look down on earth and think oneself superior to it. Western travel literature is full of descriptions of the view from on top, emphasizing how far how much can be seen, but the view lacks quality. Chinese landscape painters lifted up their eyes unto the hills. They did not look down from them.

7.

Not Living for Themselves

Heaven abides; earth lasts.
They last and abide
By not living for themselves.
Hence they live forever.

Therefore the sage
Puts himself last,
Finds himself first;
Abandons his self,
Preserves his self.
Is it not because he has no self
That he is able to realize himself?

"The first shall be last and the last shall be first." [Matthew 19:30, Moffatt] "For whoever wants to save his life will lose it, and whoever loses his life… will find it." [Matthew 16:25] The danger is self. "Beware of striving in thy own will," writes Quaker George Fox; "Thy own will is deceit." [Epistle 97, 1669] Israel ben Eliezer, founder of Hasidism, says, "The man who looks only at himself cannot but sink into despair, yet as soon as he opens his eyes to the creation around him he shall know joy." [Elie Wiesel, *Souls on Fire*, p. 26]

8.

Goodness is like Water

True goodness is like water;
Water benefits the ten thousand things
But does not compete with them.

100

It stays in places disliked by man,
Therefore comes close to Tao.

For a dwelling keep to the ground.
In your heart keep to the deeps.
In dealing with others, keep to gentleness.
In speaking, keep to truth.
In governing, keep to order.
In business, keep to efficiency.
In making moves, keep the right pace.
If you do not compete,
You will not be faulted.

Throughout the Tao Teh Ching, not competing is a corollary of not putting oneself first, a virtue that is its own reward but one that finds use in all human and natural affairs. It comes from Tao, and it leads to Tao. In China it has attracted men and women and it has also repelled men and women. If such is the case with China, whose traditional culture did not emphasize self, consider the case of the West, whose education, commerce, and culture have long been based on people putting themselves first.

9.

Hold onto Fullness?

Hold onto fullness?
It's better to stop.
Handle sharp edges?
They can't long be kept.
When gold and jade fill a house,
No one can protect it.
Pride in wealth and fame
Breeds its own collapse.

Do your work, retire:
This is the Tao of heaven.

"Seekest thou great things? Seek them not." So advises Jeremiah. [Jeremiah 45:4, King James Version] "Store up no treasures for yourselves on earth," advises Jesus, "where moth and rust corrode, where thieves break in and steal.... [F]or where your treasure lies, your heart will lie there also." [Matthew 6:19]

10.

Work but Don't Claim

In maintaining the vital spirit,
Can you hold to oneness
And not come apart?

In developing the vital senses,
Can you be like an infant child?
In clearing the inward vision,
Can you be without guilt?
In loving the people and ruling the state,
Can you hold to nothing-knowing?
In opening and closing heaven's gate,
Can you act like a mother bird?
While seeing clearly in the four directions,
Can you hold to nothing-doing?

Rear the people,
Feed the people.
Rear them but don't own them.
Work but don't claim;
Lead but don't butcher.
Call this inward virtue.

Oneness: Throughout Lao Tzŭ, oneness, wholeness, the original, and the primal are terms that refer either to Tao or to the unspoiled condition that lacks polar tensions and leads to Tao. In Tao, apparent opposites such as yin and yang do not clash but fuse.

"Can you act like a mother bird?" is often translated for purposes of clarity as "Can you act the role of the female?" Lao Tzŭ is indeed persuaded of the superior role of the so-called inferior principle, but here he uses the striking image of *mother bird* and not the symbolic manifestation of *yin* in *yang-yin*.

Virtue is the reasonably acceptable translation of the second word in the title of the Tao Teh Ching, but it does not mean a condition had by virtuous people. The word appears frequently throughout the text, in the course of which its meaning can be sensed.

11.

The Utility of Emptiness

Thirty spokes share one hub;
In emptiness lies the wheel's utility.
Kneading clay makes a pot;
In emptiness lies the pot's utility.
Cutting doors and windows makes a room;
In emptiness lies the room's utility.

Gain can be had from somethingness,
But use can be had from nothingness.

Widely valued is nothingness. When the Hasidic teacher Aaron of Karlin was asked what he had learned from his teacher, he replied, "Nothing at all." He added, "The nothing-at-all is what I learned. I learned the meaning of nothingness. I learned that I am nothing at all, and that I am notwithstanding." [*Tales*, pp. 198-199] Dov Bear of Mezritch said, "Nothing in the world can change from one thing into another unless it first turns into nothing: the primal state which no one can grasp because it is a force which precedes creation." [*Tales*, p. 104] Of like experience is Isaac Penington: "(They) feel their own poverty and nothingness.... Their way to become strong

103

in Christ is first to become weak in themselves.... [S]elf is of no reputation or value." [*Letters*, 1796 edition, pp. 25 and 30]

12.

The Belly Not the Eye

The five colors blind the eye.
The five notes deafen the ear.
The five flavors dull the taste.
Racing and hunting madden the heart.
Rare goods make men falter.

Therefore the sage
Tends the belly not the eye.
He rejects the outward,
Clasps the inward.

Outward excitements confuse inward experience. Early Quakers turned against music and dramatics because external excitement, even in those quiet times, played up and down on the emotions and made it difficult to attend inward Light. George Fox writes, "Whatsoever ye see yourselves addicted to, temptations, corruptions, uncleanness, &c,... stand still in the light that shows them to you, and then strength comes from the Lord, and help. Then you grow in peace, and no trouble shall you move." [Epistle 19, 1652]

The last two lines of this chapter, translated literally, read: "Rejects that, clasps this." Throughout the Tao Teh Ching, *that* and *this* are used synonymously for outwardness and inwardness. Translations have necessarily an introductory character, and the choice has been made to render Lao Tzŭ's *this* and *that* with their closest English equivalents in meaning. As readers' familiarity with Lao Tzŭ grows, they may wish to substitute mentally or scribble in the original terms.

13.

Favor and Disgrace

Favor and disgrace: same fear.
Honor and distress: same self.

What is meant by:
"Favor and disgrace: same fear"?
Favor makes the lowly
Fearful when they get it,
Fearful when they lose it.
That's why favor and disgrace
Are the same fear.

What is meant by:
"Honor and distress: same self"?
The self registers our distress:
If we have no self,
We have no distress.

Therefore,
He who values all things as his self
Can manage all things.
He who loves all things as his self
Can be trusted with all things.

The difficulties of translating the first two lines of this chapter give some idea of the problems of language-bridging. Literally, or as literally as they can be put down, these lines read: "Favor disgrace like fear. / Honor distress like body." Classical Chinese is as remarkable for the words it leaves out as for those it includes. Moreover, nouns are often verbs and verbs nouns. Making favor into a verb is one approach to translating the first line, but it requires additional verbiage not suggested by the original. Dr. Lin Yutang treats all the principal words as nouns, and his translation reads: "Favor and disgrace cause one dismay. / What we value and what we fear are within our self." Removing needless words produces an echo of the terseness of the original, as attempted in the first two lines above. The meaning is somewhat similar to that of the popular adage, "Praise and blame are all the same."

Self, the last word in the second line, is a translation of *shen*, usually rendered as body, although it also means person. If the word body is used in this chapter, the chapter is impenetrable. But if the word self is used, the sense of the chapter takes shape instantly. Dr. Lin uses self on the strength of a near-identical passage from Chuang Tzŭ, where the context makes the meaning evident, but there cannot be certainty as to whether this chapter means more than is evident in the "body" of it.

14.

Today's Nowness

Look at it; you can't see it:
Call it shadowless.
Listen to it; you can't hear it:
Call it soundless.
Grasp at it; you can't hold it:
Call it bodiless.

These three are beyond scrutiny;
Thus they merge into one.
Its upper side is not bright,
Its lower side not dark.
Continually the can't-be-named goes on
And comes back to nothingness.
Call it the formless form,
The imageless image,
The obscure.

From in front, you don't see its head.
From behind, you don't see its back.

106

But hold onto the Tao of old
And you can handle today's nowness.
Knowing the primal is the key to Tao.

Chapter 14 is reasonably representative of the chapters in which differences between the new Mawangtui finds and the standard Wang Pi text are frequent, and therefore gives opportunity to examine points of divergence. In his book on the new finds, a work of research and translation and interpretation that does not overreach, the author, Professor Robert G. Henricks [*Te-Tao Ching*, pp. 214-215], takes note of the following differences in the Mawangtui texts.

Adjectives in lines two and six of the first paragraph are reversed. The pronoun *this*, present in the first line of the second paragraph of the standard Wang Pi texts, is missing from the Mawangtui texts. In the third line of the same paragraph, the word *not* is emphasized by repetition. The first two lines of the last paragraph are reversed. And different particles (of the nature of grammatical assists) make possible translation of the Tao of old as the Tao of the present.

There are, in addition, other particles that do not appear in the standard text, but these do not alter sense. In other chapters, new lines occasionally appear and old ones disappear, but it can be said that differences between the texts are, as Professor Henricks notes, subtle.

15.

Concealment

Tao's ancient masters were
Inwardly subtle and darkly perceptive.
Their depth was beyond understanding.

Because they were beyond understanding,
They can be described only by appearance:
Hesitant as if wading a river in winter,
Reluctant as if fearing a neighbor,

Reserved as if acting as guest,
Effacing like ice starting to melt,
Simple like uncarved wood,
Open like a valley,
Confused like muddy water.

Who else could clear muddy water
By quieting it?
Who else could move clear water
By bringing it to life?

Whoever keeps to Tao
Does not want to be full.
Not full, he can practice
Concealment instead of accomplishment.

The characteristics of the ancient masters may make it
seem that they could have existed only in times that were
indeed ancient. The translator, however, not infrequently
met such individuals circa 1940 in the farming areas and
hill country of distant parts of China then still traditional in
culture. Among scholars, the late Chou Li-fei, to whom the
present translation owes much, was so possessed of the
qualities remarked in the above chapter that his presence
was not infrequently a source of public amazement. Some
of the characteristics may even be Western. In describing
Captain MacWhirr in *Typhoon*, Joseph Conrad managed to
combine British solidity with a manner that was reluctant,
reserved, effacing, and simple.

16.

Utmost Emptiness

Reach utmost emptiness;
Hold fast to stillness.
The ten thousand things stir about;
I only watch for their going back.

Things flourish,
But each returns to its root.
Returning to the root is peace,
And peace is a going back to reality.

To go back to reality is to be constant;
To know the constant is to find insight;
Not to know the constant is to court calamity.

To know the constant is to be broad;
To be broad is to be just.
To be just is to be universal;
To be universal is to be heavenly.
To be heavenly is to find Tao;
To find Tao is to live forever
And to rob danger from death.

Returning. Lao Tzŭ calls repeatedly for a going back or a returning to the primal, the one, the Tao. Turning to the Eternal would be a close Biblical equivalent.

George Fox advises, "Return within and wait to hear the voice of the Lord there." [Epistle 5, 1652] And Francis Howgill, an enthusiast who died in prison in 1669, says, "Why gad you abroad? Return, return to him that is the first love and the first born of every creature, who is the light of the world. Return home to within, sweep your homes; you will see the leaven that is there, the grain of mustard which the Kingdom of God is like, this you will see...." [*Works*, 1676, pp. 70-71]

Martin Buber states, "It is known that turning stands in the center of the Hasidic conception of the way of man. But turning means here something much greater than repentance and acts of penance; it means that by a reversal of his whole being, a man who has been lost in a maze of selfishness, where he has always set himself as his goal, finds a way to God, that is, a way to the fulfillment of the particular task for which he, this particular man, has been destined by God.... No soul has its object in itself, in its own salvation." [*The Way of Man*, pp. 25 and 26]

The second and third paragraphs seem to be of a chain-argument character, but this is probably a stylistic rather than a substantive consideration, the argument having psychological links. See commentary for Chapter 59.

Universal. In the line, "To be universal is to be heavenly," the character for universal is usually translated as king, long its common meaning. But some of the commentators have held that *universal* was one of its ancient meanings. The translator has taken advantage of their opinion because the word king excludes in particular women. While Lao Tzǔ makes frequent use of the word man, in Chinese a generic term for human being regardless of sex, Lao Tzǔ is not patriarchal (in this he is unlike Confucius) and tends to favor the maternal. Among writers of the Bronze Age, when patriarchy completely overcame the matrilocalism of the New Stone Age, he was the one known feminist.

Reality. In the line, "And peace is a going back to reality," the character translated as reality is usually translated as destiny. It can also mean life. Reality embraces both meanings.

17.

The Ruler Unknown

Of the best ruler,
The people only know that he exists.
Next comes one they love and praise.
Next comes one they fear.
Next comes one they abhor.
When you are lacking in trust,
Others have no trust in you.
Of the work of one
Who is short with his words,
The hundred families say:
We have done it ourselves.

"If you do not trust, you will not be trusted." [Isaiah 7:9, translated by Martin Buber, *Two Types*, p. 28] Isaiah's first emphasis is on being trusted by the Eternal, whereas Lao Tzŭ's emphasis is on being trusted by all Creation, but these meanings embrace one another so closely as to include each other. Both present the relationship of trust as a reality of life and not as the whim of a man-resembling deity.

As for rulers, Lao Tzŭ is certain that he who rules least rules best, but always with the caveat that no one rules well unless Tao rules him. Central to the Tao Teh Ching is the perception that life is too complicated to be managed effectively and that it must be let to happen, but this perception is based on one still deeper, that eternal Tao, not transient greed or other aspects of human will, alone makes such nothing-doing fruitful.

18.

Great Hypocrites

> When Tao is cast aside,
> Duty and humanity abide.
> When prudence and wit appear,
> Great hypocrites are here.
>
> When the six relations have no point,
> Filial piety and paternal love are taught.
> When the countryside is out of joint,
> Loyal officials are man's lot.

We are not the dogs of God but his children. Prophetic religion has to do with relationships not observances, with awe not belief, with love not guilt, with life not property, with the Way not moralism. Obedience to the Way is of great use only if freely given, of little use or no use if it is in any way compelled.

The term *six relations* included those relationships

111

around which the lives of Chinese families had long centered: parent and child, older child and younger child, and husband and wife.

The liberties taken to produce rhyming lines involve no actual changes in meaning. In more literal translation, *are here* would read *abide*, *have no point* would read *are out of order*, *taught* would read *preached*, and *are man's lot* would read *abide*.

19.

Reduce the Self

Give up wisdom,
Abandon knowledge,
And the people will
Benefit a hundredfold.
Give up benevolence,
Abandon righteousness,
And the people will
Go back to natural affection.
Give up cunning,
Abandon gain,
And robbers and thieves
Will disappear.

External rules are not enough;
Hold to what can be counted on:
Keep to simplicity,
Grasp the primal,
Reduce the self,
And curb desire.

In giving up righteousness, Hasidism provides a long and progressive history of treating the very piety to which it was wholeheartedly devoted as an obstacle to man's relationship with God and with man. "Being pious," said Pinhas of Koretz, "I prefer to being clever, but I prefer being good to being clever and to being pious." Several generations later, a teacher from the school of Karlin said, "Cleverness without heart is nothing; pious means false." In the sixth generation, Bunan of Pshysha said, "If someone is merely good, he is a debauched lover; if he is merely pious, he is a thief; if he is merely clever, he is a disbeliever." [*Hasidism*, pp. 166-167]

Martin Buber comments: "Whoever surrenders himself to a vague kind of love without accepting faith and wisdom will lose himself in bewilderment like one debauched. Whoever desires to confine himself to an emotional relationship to God without perceiving the living world around him robs mankind of what belongs to it. And he who... is attached to God only by the ties of (traditional) religion and morals... will lose even that weak hold which these external ties provide. Wholeness is reliable and leads man to God." [*Hasidism*, pp. 167-168]

"What we must beware of is this persistent discrimination between ourselves and our neighbor, the conceit of discrimination, the deception of discrimination—indeed, this entire triumphal world of illusion, based upon a self-satisfying discrimination.... Raphael of Bershad said in the last summer before his death, 'We must now lay aside all pious deeds so that there will be no more estrangement.' " [*Hasidism*, pp. 181-182] To get Tao, to follow the Way, abandon righteousness!

The first twelve lines of this chapter indicate outward obstacles to the inwardness of the last six lines, which in turn show how these obstacles can be overcome.

20.

Mild, Stupid, Dull, Low, Uncouth

> Give up learning:
> Have no anxieties.
> How much difference is there
> Between ah and oh?

How much difference is there
Between good and evil?
What men fear
Must I fear?
Utter nonsense!

All men are happy happy,
As if consuming sacrificial feasts,
As if mounting the Spring Terrace.
I alone am mild,
Like one who gives no sign,
Like an infant who does not smile,
Forlorn, forlorn,
Like one with no place to go.

All men have plenty;
I alone am a loser,
A fool at heart indeed!
And stupid stupid!
The world's people are bright bright;
I alone am dull dull.
The world's people are smart smart;
I alone am low low,
Bland as the sea,
Aimless as the wind.

All men have their uses;
I alone am stubborn and uncouth.
But I differ most from the others
In prizing food drawn from my Mother.

What men fear / Must I fear? In similar mood, Isaiah [9:12]
thunders against the worldly, the popular and conventional.

Do not call out "Danger!"
  when this people calls out "Danger!"
Have no fear of what they fear;
  never dread it.

The meaning of *Spring Terrace* is no longer certain.

A loser / A fool at heart indeed! John Woolman writes, "I find that to be a fool as to worldly wisdom and commit my cause to God, not fearing to offend men who take offense at the simplicity of Truth, is the only way to remain unmoved at the sentiments of others." [*Journal*, 1756]

Stupid stupid, dull dull. It is said that "What is hidden from the wise and learned is revealed to the simple minded." [Matthew 12:25] Prophetic religion is of the people, not of the intelligentsia.

Prizing food drawn from my Mother. Mother refers, as it does throughout Lao Tzŭ, to Tao. Tao is neuter as God is neuter, but Tao is feminine as God is masculine.

21.

Elusive, Evasive

The nature of great virtue
Is to follow Tao alone.
And Tao's style is elusive, evasive.
Evasive, elusive,
Yet within it is form.
Elusive, evasive,
Yet within it is substance,
Dark and dim,
Yet within it is vitality.
Its vitality is very real:
Within it is trust.

From of old
Its name has not ceased,
For it has watched all beginnings.
How can all beginnings be watched?
Inward Light!

Prophetic religions are religions of the Way. They call for a manner of living, not for a set of formal beliefs or

115

prescribed actions, a manner that is grounded in the Way itself and open to its awesomeness. The book of Psalms reverberates with the cries of people who turn to God: "Let me see thy ways, O thou Eternal, teach me what are thy paths." [Psalm 25:4] "Teach me what is thy way, O thou Eternal, and lead me by a level road." [Psalm 27:11] Martin Buber comments, "We may say that God wills that man should choose Him and not fall away from Him, but we have to add that God also wills that His creation shall not be an end in itself, but a way; that His world shall be a way; and more than that: in order that this may be so in reality, He wills that his creatures shall go the way themselves, they must be in their own persons, from out of their own personalities...." [*Hasidism*, p. 109]

Quaker historian Rufus Jones says, "Quakerism at its birth was a fresh attempt to recover the way of life revealed in the New Testament, to reinterpret and relive it in this present world. Its founders intended to revive apostolic Christianity. They did not intend to create a new sect." [Friends World Conference, 1937, Report]

Inward Light! The original exclaims tersely, "By this!" (See commentary to Chapter 12.) The term used here and in Chapters 12, 54, and 57 is one of numerous phrases common among the early Quakers (including the Way) and described by George Fox, following the Gospel of John, as the light which "hath enlightened every man that cometh into the world withal...." [*Journal*, 1648]

22.

Twist and Get Whole

Twist and get whole.
Bend and get straight.
Be empty and get filled.
Be worn and get renewed.
Have little: get much.
Have much: get baffled.

Therefore the sage
Holds to the One and
Becomes beneath-heaven's pattern.
He does not show himself,
Hence he shines;
Does not assert himself,
Hence he is seen;
Does not boast his merits,
Hence he gets credit;
Does not vaunt himself,
Hence he survives;
Does not compete with anyone,
Hence no one beneath heaven
Can compete with him.

The old saying,
The twisted shall be made whole,
Is no empty phrase.
Be whole and you will return.

How apposite are opposites! The tone of the first paragraph is the tone of the later Isaiah [40:14], who says "Every valley shall be exalted, and every mountain shall be made low: and the crooked shall be made straight, and the rough places plain."

Moreover, in both tone and content, the first paragraph is similar to the beatitudes of the first gospel, which [in Matthew 5:3-8] read as follows:

Blessed are those who feel poor in spirit!
    the Realm of Heaven is theirs.
Blessed are the mourners!
    they will be consoled.
Blessed are the humble!
    they will inherit the earth.
Blessed are those who hunger and thirst for goodness!
    they will be satisfied.

117

These observations, whether uttered by Jesus or Lao Tzŭ, have little to do with the precepts and strictures of conventional religion. They are in no way theological. What they describe is not what will be or what ought to be or what is thought to be, but that which, in the inward areas of man's being, indisputably is and which, in the outward areas of social life, comes about as it comes about.

Between the themes of the second and third paragraphs of Chapter 22—between, that is, selflessness and wholeness—there is a clear inward connection. The whole to which the twisted return is exemplified in a passage in Deuteronomy which Martin Buber translates as "Thou shall be entire (undivided) with YHVH thy God." [Deuteronomy 18:13, *Two Types*, p. 61] To be entire is "to worship the Eternal your God with all your mind and all your heart." [Deuteronomy 10:12, Moffatt] To these words Leviticus adds, "Love your neighbor as one like yourself." [Leviticus 19:18, Buber: *Between*, p. 51] To Lao Tzŭ, however, love of God and man may be not so much the total sum of wholeness as one of the characteristics of it.

23.

No Fuss

Nature speaks little.
Squalls do not last the morning
Nor downpours the day.
What stirs them up?
Heaven-and-earth!
Even heaven-and-earth
Does not long make a fuss.
How much less should men!

Therefore,
He who follows Tao
Is one with Tao.

118

He who follows virtue
Is one with virtue.
He who follows loss
Is one with his losses.
Virtue is glad to get
Whatever comes to virtue.
Loss is glad to get
Whatever comes to loss.

When you are lacking in trust,
Others will have no trust in you.

24.

Tumors and Dregs

On tiptoe you don't stand.
Astride you don't walk.
Showing yourself, you don't shine.
Asserting yourself, you don't show.
Boasting yourself won't get you credit.
Vaunting yourself won't let you endure.

In Tao, these things are called
Tumors and dregs, which all things abhor.
Whoever has Tao does not dwell on them.

In the last half of the seventeenth century, Pinhas of Koretz made much the same point when he said, "What you pursue, you don't get. But what you allow to grow slowly in its own way, comes to you." [*Hasidism*, p. 129]

25.

Tao Follows Itself

Something there is
Without form and complete,

Born before heaven and earth,
Solitary and vast,
Standing alone without change.
Everywhere pervading all things,
Mothering all beneath heaven.
I don't know its name;
I style it Tao,
And for want of a name call it great.
To be great is to go on.
To go on is to be far.
To be far is to return.

Therefore,
Tao is great.
Heaven is great.
Earth is great.
Man also is great.
The universe has four greats,
And man is one of them.

Man follows earth;
Earth follows heaven;
Heaven follows Tao;
Tao follows itself.

In different words but in like mood is the later Isaiah's song of enveloping and overwhelming awe over the works of Creation, part of which [40:21-23, 28-29] reads:

Can you not understand, cannot you see?
Were you not told this from the first,
have you not grasped this,
since the world began?—
that He sits over the round earth, so high
that its inhabitants look like grasshoppers;
he spreads the skies out like a curtain,
and stretches them out like a tent....
Come now! do you not understand,

have you not heard,
that the Eternal is an everlasting God?
the maker of the world from end to end?
He never faints, never is weary,
his insight is unsearchable;
into the weary he puts power,
and adds new strength to the weak.

The paragraphs from Lao Tzŭ, not less than the passages from Isaiah, are songs of praise to the wonder of the creator and to the essential goodness of his creation. Unlike those faiths which view material creation as evil and food as at best an unpleasant necessity, and which hold that spiritual escape from both is good, the Tao Teh Ching is profoundly physical and profoundly affirmative, considering good Creation's every aspect, as does the first chapter of Genesis with its mighty refrain, "And God saw that it was good."

In the next-to-last paragraph, in which man is called one of the four greats, the translator has rendered as *man* a character usually rendered as *king*. (See commentary to Chapter 16.) Some commentaries suggest that the word *king* includes and even symbolizes *man*. In the last paragraph, however, the character used for *man* has always meant man.

26.

He Does Not Stir But Sits

The heavy is the root of the light.
The still is the master of the restless.

Therefore,
The sage travels all day,
But never leaves the baggage wagon.
Though there are arresting sights,
He does not stir but sits.

> Why does the master
> Of ten thousand chariots
> Show levity to all beneath heaven?
> Levity will uproot him,
> Restlessness unman him.

How narrowing is travel! The sage prefers to sit rather than to move, and if he must move, he declines to chase about after exciting sights. (See also Chapter 47.) Indeed, the farther he goes, the less he knows.

The first and second paragraphs of this chapter may appear unrelated, but the master of ten thousand chariots is simply an early Chinese version of the world traveler who insists on seeing all and ends by sensing nothing.

The first and fifth lines above provide one of the numerous puns—not light puns but heavy ones—that surpass the measuring scales of translators. Heaviness is the quality that overcomes levity in line one, while it is the last of two characters for baggage wagon: *wagon heavy*.

27.

The Subtle Secret

> Good walkers leave no marks to track;
> Good speakers leave no nits to pick.
> Good reckoners use no computers.
> Good lockers turn no keys,
> Yet no one opens their locks.
> Good binders tie no ropes,
> Yet no one undoes their knots.
>
> What is more,
> The sage is always good at saving people:
> No one is cast out.
> He is also good at saving things:
> No thing is cast out.
> Call this following the light.

Hence good men teach the not-good.
Not-good men are the lessons of the good.
Not to esteem the teacher,
Not to love the lesson,
Is to go astray despite great learning.
Call this the subtle secret.

Paragraph one suggests that the way to solve problems is to avoid outward devices and clever plans. Paragraph two, however, seems to speak only of the obvious, something with little connection to either paragraph one or paragraph three. And the final paragraph is little more than Confucian in its conventional attachment to learning, unless the subtle secret is that good men should esteem not-good men as mentors just as not-good men should esteem them.

The temptation in reading scripture is to attribute anything out of key (or, indeed, anything less than excellent) to later additions or corruptions. This ploy probably should be resisted, simply because no one can know with any certainty what may be an addition or a corruption and what may not be. To repeat, it may be wiser to disregard whatever in scripture fails to speak to one's condition than to attempt to rationalize it. The whole book is the best key to its parts.

28.

Masculine/Feminine

Know the masculine;
Keep to the feminine.
Be beneath-heaven's ravine.
To be beneath-heaven's ravine
Is to stay with unceasing virtue
And to return to infancy.

Know the white;
Keep to the black.

123

Be beneath-heaven's model.
To be beneath-heaven's model
Is to stay with unerring virtue
And return to the limitless.

Know the glorious;
Keep to disgrace.
Be beneath-heaven's valley.
To be beneath-heaven's valley
Is to stay with constant virtue
And return again to simplicity.

When simplicity diversifies
It produces instruments
That the sage uses as officers.
Indeed, a great leader
Does little cutting.

It is through lowness and passivity, Lao Tzŭ declares, that simplicity and humility become great social goods, as suggested but not said in the final paragraph.

Ravine and *valley* are words synonymous with lowliness. (They are also, as noted earlier, better places from which to enjoy mountains than are high places.)

Infancy refers to a state of wholeness.

White and *black*, the colors of yin and yang, are symbols for the masculine and the feminine.

Simplicity. This word can also be rendered as uncarved wood, a Taoist synonym for it, but use of this alternate does not make the meaning of the final paragraph notably clearer. If the first sentence is made to read, "When uncarved wood is broken up (or sawed up or cut up)," it seems to stand in opposition to the last sentence, "A great leader does little cutting." Leader can also be rendered as cutter, thereby producing a Taoist-sounding aphorism but without contributing more sense to the paragraph. Here the translator has sought to be literal, not suggestive. See the final note to the preceding chapter.

29.

Acting

Does anyone want to take the world
And act on it?
I don't see how he can succeed.
The world is a sacred vessel
Not to be acted on.
Whoever acts on it spoils it;
Whoever grasps at it loses it.

Indeed, there is a time
For some things to go forward
And some to go behind;
Some to blow hot,
And some to blow cold;
Some to grow in strength,
And some to decay;
Some to be up,
And some to be down.

Therefore the sage eschews
Excesses, extremes, and extravagances.

In paragraph one, *world*—typically used in translating Lao Tzŭ—is here used instead of the literal *beneath heaven*.

The phrase *there is a time / For* does not appear in the text, but it has the blessing of commentators, most of them necessarily unaware of resemblances to Ecclesiastes 3.

The fulsome sounds of the last two lines, the work of Dr. John Wu, match the impact of the original characters.

30.

Bad Harvests, Big Wars

He who uses Tao to guide rulers
Does not force beneath-heaven with arms.
Such things recoil on their users.

Where armies are
Briars and brambles grow.
Bad harvests follow big wars.
Be firm and that is all:
Dare not rely on force.
Be firm but not haughty,
Firm but not boastful,
Firm but not proud,
Firm when necessary,
Firm but non-violent.

Things that flourish
Fall into decay.
This is not-Tao,
And what is not-Tao
Soon ends.

God is not out of this world! Neither is Tao! Lao Tzŭ does not propose beyond-creation ecstasy of any sort; he does not even mention anything similar to it, although this device for escaping everyday reality to serve self was not uncommon in his times. Perhaps it was as common as it is in ours. The Tao Teh Ching is continually concerned with the mundane, with the social: the areas in which Tao is to be followed. The Way is to be followed, Chapter 30 declares, amid the hard realities of wars.

Lao Tzŭ may not have precise certainty as to how, in history's early morning, violence is to be overcome, but he knows certainly that it is clearly not-Tao, "and what is not-Tao soon ends." In like manner, Isaiah knows violence to be clearly an offense against God:

Your hands are full of bloodshed;
wash yourselves clean,
banish your evil doings
   from my sight,
cease to do wrong,
learn to do right,

126

make justice all your aim,
and put a check on violence.
[Isaiah 1:15-17]

God is here-and-now. Martin Buber writes, "An immediate relation to God which does not embody an immediate
relation to the world is self deception.... [Y]ou are not
concentrating on the reality of God but merely on your
own idea of Him. The religious element in isolation is not
really the religious element." [*Hasidism*, p. 167]

31.

Tools of Ill Fortune

Fine weapons are tools of ill fortune;
All things seem to hate them.
Whoever has Tao does not depend on them.

At home a gentleman favors the left;
In war he favors the right.
Since weapons are tools of ill fortune,
They are not tools for a gentleman,
Who uses them only from necessity.
Peace and quiet he upholds;
Victory he does not enjoy.
To enjoy victory is to like slaughter.
Whoever likes it
Cannot thrive beneath heaven.

Things of good omen favor the left:
Things of ill omen favor the right.
The under-general stands to the left;
The top-general stands to the right:
The way to stand at a burial rite.
Killing multitudes brings weeping and sorrow;
Treat victory like a funeral.

Whoever has Tao does not depend upon weapons. He uses them, says Lao Tzŭ, "only from necessity," but Lao Tzŭ appears to admit of their being used. In like manner, Isaiah has visions of a peaceable kingdom, but he does not directly interdict warfare in a land that is far from peaceability. Consistency is not the issue here; precise consistency is the preoccupation of persons who wish to display the ideological purity of their own selves. Nor is the absence of specific planning for peace an issue: outward plans have a disturbing propensity for stirring conflict. The issue is whether there is a Way or a Realm upon which to depend, not simply for the partial, but for the ultimate conquest, however slow, of violence and oppression. The issue is whether to have faith or not to have faith, to trust or not to trust in the Way creation is created. Isaiah and Lao Tzŭ trust. This early trust in the Way of peace remains the solid and lasting basis for all subsequent testimony against violence.

The left is the honorable side, *the right* the less honorable side.

The last paragraph of this chapter has been called a later addition, possibly a marginal gloss that crept into the text. There was no such military title as under-general until the Han dynasty, which began in 206 B.C. The buried Mawangtui text, however, could not have been tampered with, and it too contains the words *under general*. Evidently the change in the Mawangtui and the standard texts resulted not from a gloss but from the use of a new term that became current between 206 and 168 B.C.

32.

No Names

Tao is always without name,
Simple and small.
Beneath-heaven dares not subject it.

If kings and barons can hold to it,
The ten thousand things will pay homage.
Heaven and earth will mutually join,
And sweet dew will fall.
Not by law but of themselves
The people will stay in balance.

When law and order arose,
Names appeared.
Aren't there enough already?
Is it not time to stop?
To know when to stop
Is to be free from danger.

Tao is to all beneath heaven
As rivers and seas are to
Rivulets and streams.

No names! They are devices used by the human mind to get the better of creation by cogitating it and trying to explain it. They are devices used by oppressors who force life into molds and by the learned who try to identify the molds. Tao is without name and is identifiable chiefly as a path. YHVH is without name, and is identifiable chiefly as presence: the Everpresent who still says, "I will be there."

Lao Tzŭ's testimony against names is of course a testimony against conceptualizing life and of worshiping the concept (or the conceptualizer) instead of Tao. But it is also a testimony against Bronze and Stone Age superstition, then rife, and suggests that superstition's roots may not be entirely distinguishable from those of science.

There is no need for names if nature is accepted and not feared. To fear it is to control it. Should it be feared? The gospel of Matthew [6:26, 28-29] reads:

Look at the wild birds;
they sow not, they reap not;

129

they gather nothing in granaries,
and yet your heavenly Father feeds them.
Look how the lilies of the field grow;
they neither toil nor spin,
and yet, I tell you, even Solomon
in all his grandeur was never
robed like one of them.

Despite the notion that all comparable things have a common origin, it is impossible that the Tao Teh Ching influenced first century Judea. Prophetic religion springs from something other than cultural interchange!

33.

Whoever

Whoever knows others has wisdom;
Whoever knows himself has insight.
Whoever conquers others has force;
Whoever conquers himself has strength.
Whoever knows he has enough has wealth.
Whoever perseveres has purpose.
Whoever keeps to one place endures.
Whoever dies without perishing lives long.

Nothing fanciful is contained in any of these terse exclamations of early Taoist experience. When Lao Tzŭ writes that "whoever knows he has enough has wealth" (as he writes in various parts of the Tao Teh Ching), he is not phrasing or exploring the topic of non-attachment. Rather he is reporting that awareness of the everyday reality of *enough* produces a simplicity of living that is wealth, whereas possession and money produce no such thing.

The idea of dying without perishing is much less clear. Early Taoism embraces deathlessness, but not a self-produced type of it suggested by this chapter's last line. Look here for sense, not meaning.

34.

Call It Small, Call It Great

The great Tao flows everywhere:
It can go to the right or the left.
The ten thousand things draw life from it,
And it does not deny them.

It completes its work
But takes no title.
It clothes and feeds the ten thousand things
But does not own them.
You can call it small.
The ten thousand things return to it,
But it does not own them.
You can call it great.

Because it does not seek to be great,
Its greatness is accomplished.

Entirely different in word and entirely similar in tone is the exclamation of the Psalmist: [Psalm 85:10]

Better a single day within thy courts
than a thousand days outside!
I would rather sit at the threshold
    of God's house
than live in the tents of worldly men.

Like the Psalmist, Lao Tzŭ's word is not to emulate Tao, whereby man would aim to resemble the Most High (or in early Taoist language the Most Low), but rather to follow Tao and, in the language of another world, do its will. The omnipresence of Tao does not arise from the nature of worship but from a sense of the majestic reality of the One. It could even be said that the heavens declare the glory of Tao, that the firmament showeth its handiwork, and that there is no place where its voice is not heard.

35.

Tao is Bland

Hold to the great symbol:
All beneath heaven will follow,
Follow without harm,
Quiet, even, secure.

Music and dainties
Make passing guests pause.
But Tao is bland and without taste.
Looked at, it can't be seen;
Listened to, it can't be heard;
Used, it can't be used up.

More communicative than the word is not any word at all. Without quiet there is no evenness, no security, for only in unspoken response do people unite one with another and reach out to Tao. More attractive, also, than the attractive is the simple, which is beyond hearing and seeing. Jesus quotes Isaiah: [Matthew 13:14]

You will hear and hear and never understand,
You will see and see and never perceive.

Lao Tzŭ's outcry against learning has much to do with the desire of the clever to see more than eyes can simply see and hear more than ears can simply hear. Jesus, it may well be recalled, praised God "for hiding all this from the wise and learned and revealing it to the simple-minded." [Matthew 11:25] Tao too tolerates fools.

36.

The Subtle Truth

What is going to shrink has first been stretched.
What is going to weaken has first been made strong.

What is going to be ruined has first been raised up.
What is going to be taken away has first been given.
Call this the subtle truth:
The soft and weak conquer the hard and strong.

Fish should not leave the depths;
Neither should weapons of state ever be aired.

Lao Tzŭ offers no pap for innocents, no balm for hermits.
Despite the notion of some scholars of times past that he
was an anonymous and impractical quietest, his first topic
is governing. In the course of the Sino-Japanese war,
a reformist prime minister who met strong resistance from
his fellow ministers found that he had to strengthen his
position by taking lessons in the Tao Teh Ching. The *way*
things are done can be more important than what is done.

37.

Everything Gets Done

Tao never does anything,
And everything gets done.
If a ruler can keep to it,
The ten thousand things
Will change of themselves.

Changed, things may stir desire.
Quiet them with the nameless simple,
Which alone brings no-desire.
No desire: then there is peace,
And beneath heaven
Will settle down of itself.

The Mawangtui finds do not contain in this chapter or in
Chapter 48 the familiar do-nothing do-everything paradox that appears in the standard text. Some experts,
possibly of non-paradoxical bent, have taken the oppor-

133

tunity to suggest that do-nothing do-everything was not part of the original text but rather a later addition. Professor Henricks' Mawangtui book, sound and balanced, indicates that the new manuscripts have gaps due to age at these points, suggesting that the paradoxes were present in the manuscripts' original form.

38.

When Tao Is Lost

High virtue is not virtuous;
Therefore it has virtue.
Low virtue is always virtuous;
Therefore it has no virtue.
High virtue does nothing
And has no ulterior ends.
Low virtue does something,
Also has ulterior ends.

High humanity has ulterior ends,
But it does something.
High morality does something,
Also has ulterior ends.
High ceremony does something,
And when it gets no response
It rolls up its sleeve and takes to force.

When Tao is lost, there is virtue.
When virtue is lost, there is humanity.
When humanity is lost, there is morality.
When morality is lost, there is ceremony.
Now ceremony is the shell of
Loyalty and trust
And the beginning of befuddlement.
As to foreknowledge,
It is a blossomy path
And the beginning of folly.

Therefore,
The fulfilled man holds to
The solid rather than the shell,
The fruit rather than the blossom.
He avoids the outward, accepts the inward.

The lowest level which the descending argument of this chapter reaches is that of foreknowledge. By this term, Lao Tzŭ appears to mean superstition of the self-willed sort that seeks to fulfill personal desires. He does not mean that activity which Westerners associate with the prophets of Israel, and which the Tao Teh Ching closely resembles in inward style. It is well to recall that the prophets of Israel shared a marked distrust for the sort of prophecy that deals in prediction and roundly denounced the dealers. Probably the latter were hangers-on of the court. Of them Isaiah wrote when he declared, "When they tell you to consult mediums and ghosts that cheep and gibber in low murmurs, ask them if a nation should not rather consult its God." [Isaiah 8:19]

Some generations later, Ezekiel called the word of God against the same crowd: "O Israel, your prophets are like jackals, burrowing among the ruins!... [M]y hand shall be against the prophets who see false visions and utter lying oracles." [Ezekiel 13:4, 13:9] Clearly, if those who call themselves prophets cannot be prophets, true prophets are those who do not claim to be such. The true prophets were persons so wholly turned to Truth—to the Way of it and the Word of it—that they became intimate with it and sought to establish it rather than convention as the ongoing force of daily life. Convention fares no better in the hands of Lao Tzŭ than in their hands. The prophetic is not the worldly.

A blossomy path. Compare the English usage of *the primrose path.* In early Taoist usage blossom suggests outwardness and fading. Note its use in the third paragraph and the parallelism between its use there and in the final paragraph.

135

39.

Oneness

From of old,
There are those who reached oneness:
Heaven reached oneness and became clear;
Earth reached oneness and became tranquil;
Spirits reached oneness and became mystic;
Valleys reached oneness and became full;
The ten thousand things reached oneness
And became potent;
Barons and kings reached oneness
And became sovereign.
Did they not all become so
Through oneness?

If heaven were not clear,
It probably would crack.
If earth were not tranquil,
It probably would quake.
If spirits were not mystic,
They probably would desist.
If the valleys were not full,
They probably would die out.
If ten thousand things were not potent,
They probably would die off.
If barons and kings were not sovereign,
They probably would fall.

For the great has its roots in the humble;
The high has its foundation upon the low.
Barons and kings call themselves
The orphaned, the lonely, the unworthy:
Do they not have roots in the humble?

Truly,
The parts of a cart are not the cart.
Do not shine like jade
Or sound like stone chimes.

The parts of a cart are indeed not the cart because the whole is greater than the sum of its parts. A meeting of persons, each of whom seeks the Way, finds more than the total found by the individual persons, an experience much later reported by Quaker writers.

Jade is a wondrous jewel but it jades; *stone chimes* are advanced instruments of ancient music but they emit only tinkles.

40.

Being Born of Non-being

Returning is the motion of Tao;
Softness is the utility of Tao.
All things in heaven and earth
Are born of being;
Being is born of non-being.

Returning is the motion of Tao. Of his own returning (an experience common among early Quakers), Isaac Penington writes, "But now I have been so tossed and tumbled, melted and new moulded, that I am changed into that which I thought it utterly impossible for me ever to be.... In this state of folly, I find a new state of things arising in me." [*Light or Darknesse*, 1650] In the eighteenth century, the word among the Hasidim for this state of things was *turning*. Pinhas of Koretz, for example, declared that the wicked who turn to God honor him more completely than the righteous who see no need to turn. [*Tales*, p. 127]

Being is born of non-being. Shneur Zalman of Ladi said, "All I can see is the divine nothingness which gives life to the world." [*Tales*, p. 271]

41.

Without Name and Hidden

When a superior man hears about Tao,
He goes after it diligently.
When an average man hears about Tao,
He both gets it and loses it.
When an inferior man hears about Tao,
He laughs loudly at it.
If he did not laugh,
It would not be Tao.

There is an old saying:
The bright way looks dark;
The forward way looks backward;
The smooth way looks rough;
High virtue looks low;
Great whiteness looks defiled;
Broad virtue looks deficient;
Solid virtue looks illicit;
Simple virtue looks decayed.
Great space has no corners.
Great talent ripens late.
Great music is out of key.
The great symbol is out of shape.

Tao is without name and hidden.
Hence Tao helps and completes.

Dr. Lin Yutang, who held that Chapter 41 was the best place to divide the text into upper and lower divisions, illustrated the chapter with one of Chuang Tzǔ's imaginary stories [7:10], which can be adapted thus:

Yang Chu met Lao Tzǔ on the road, and the latter turned his head to the sky and sighed, saying, "I thought you could be my disciple. Now I know you cannot."

Later Yang Chu said, "May I ask what is my fault?" Lao Tzǔ said, "You have that haughty look. Who would want to be in the same room with you? The bright way looks dark; the smooth way looks backward." Yang Chu's countenance changed.

When he left his house to see Lao Tzŭ, his people used to make way for him. They left the mat for him, and the cook left the stove. When he returned, the people in the house mingled freely with him.

42.

Perishing by Violence

Tao bore one, one bore two, two bore three;
Three bore the ten thousand things.
The ten thousand things
Carry yin and embrace yang,
Whose blending breaths make them harmonize.

Men hate to be
Orphaned, lowly, unworthy,
Yet barons and kings
Use these names as titles.
Indeed,
You may gain by losing,
And you may lose by gaining.

What others have taught, I also teach:
Men of violence perish by it.
Whoever said this is
Father of my teaching.

One, two, three. Explanations are so numerous that it is advisable to seek no explanation at all.

Gain by losing. This passage is reminiscent of Jesus' saying about losing one's life by saving it and saving one's life by losing it.

Men of violence perish by it. The saying of Jesus is that

139

"all they that take to the sword shall perish by the sword."
[Matthew 26:52 KJV] Who taught whom? The Way.

43.

Soft Overcomes Hard

The softest things beneath heaven
Overcome the hardest.
Nothingness alone penetrates no-space.
Hence I know the use
Of nothing-doing.

The lesson of nothing-speaking,
The use of nothing-doing:
Rare attainments beneath heaven!

Nothingness alone penetrates no-space. Dov Bear of Mezritch says, "He who thinks nothing at all of himself and
makes himself nothing, grows spiritual, and spirit does not
occupy space. He can be north and south at the same
time…. You must cease to be aware of yourselves. You
must be nothing but an ear which hears what the universe
of the Word is constantly saying within you. The moment
you start hearing what you yourself are saying, you must
stop." [*Tales*, pp. 107, 109]

44.

Can You Long Last

Name and self, which is dearer?
Self and wealth, which is nearer?
Gain and loss, which hurts the worst?
For:
Attachment comes at wasteful cost;
Hoarding leads to certain loss;
Knowing what is enough avoids disgrace;

Knowing when to stop secures from peril.
Only thus can you long last.

Attachment comes at wasteful cost. Martin Buber speaks of "the lust for overrunning reality. Instead of making reality the starting point of his life, full as it is of harsh contradictions,... man submits to illusion, becomes intoxicated with it, surrenders his life to it, and in the very measure in which he does this the core of his existence becomes burning and unfruitful, he becomes at once completely stimulated and in his motive power crippled." [*Hasidism*, p. 39] This attachment obviously extends to possessions and intoxicants, but it also extends to activities undertaken to prop up jerry-built edifices of self, such as great but self-serving causes speciously experienced as self-transcending and self-transforming.

Of late, non-attachment has become a popular phrase among Westerners since it suggests a rationalization for distrusting other persons and avoiding intimacy with them. Such aloofness and rationalization of it are, of course, simply constituent forms of attachment to self.

45.

Clearness

What is most perfect seems imperfect,
But using it doesn't use it up.
What is most full seems empty,
But using it doesn't wear it down.

Great straightness seems crooked;
Great skill seems clumsy,
Great eloquence seems hesitant.
Movement conquers cold,
But stillness conquers heat.

Clearness and serenity
Are beneath-heaven's norm.

All of the Tao Teh Ching necessarily suffers from observations upon it, even though such may be needful as an introduction. Chapter 45 is so full and complete that comment is useless and (what may be worse) unaesthetic. The Tao Teh Ching is not to be pondered but to be tasted. If the taste is unfamiliar, read again and again. If it seems familiar, read particularly again and again.

46.

War Horses

> When beneath-heaven has Tao,
> Race horses are used to fertilize fields.
> When beneath-heaven has no Tao,
> War horses breed in the suburbs.
>
> No calamity is greater
> Than not knowing what is enough,
> No fault worse than wanting too much.
> Whoever knows what is enough has enough.

Knowing what is enough. Yehiel Mikhal of Zlotchov says, "My life was blessed in that I never needed anything until I had it." He was asked, "…[H]ow can you pray day after day, 'Blessed be thou who has supplied my every want'? For surely you lack everything a man is in need of." He replied, "My want is, most likely, poverty, and that is what I have been supplied with." [*Tales*, pp. 138, 156]

Mohandas Gandhi declares that "Money renders a man hopeless.… If [a man] is a sane man like me, he would reach with me the conclusion that to be really happy he must not own anything or own things only so long as his neighbors permit him." [*Young India,* 1928]

John Woolman proposes that men and women mutually keep "to that spirit and power which teaches us to be content with things really needful and to avoid all superfluities." [*Journal,* 1759]

47.

No Go

Without going out of the door
You can know beneath-heaven.
Without looking out of the window
You can see heaven's way.
The farther you go,
The less you know.

Thus the sage
Knows without walking,
Sees without looking,
And does without doing.

The farther you go, / The less you know. George Fox says, "There is a great danger too in traveling in the world," the danger being self-conceit. He advises a prompt return home. [Address to Friends in the Ministry, 1667] When tempted to travel, imitate Fox and walk.

Martin Buber writes, as if in amplification of Fox, "There is something that can be found only in one place. It is a great treasure, which may be called the fulfillment of existence. The place where this treasure can be found is the place where one stands." [*Way of Man*, p. 29]

The first six lines of this chapter on the futility of travel follow Dr. Wu's felicitous phrasing closely.

48.

Subtract!

To get learning, add to it daily.
To get Tao, subtract daily.
Subtract and subtract
Until you achieve nothing-doing.
Do nothing-doing
And everything will get done.

To win beneath-heaven
Always avoid fussing.
If fussing is not avoided,
Beneath-heaven is not won.

Do nothing-doing and everything will get done. Once proverbial in China, this saying reads in romanized Chinese, *Wu wei erh wu pu wei*, literally "Not act therefore not not-act." While there remained continuity in Chinese culture, this sentence was a typical answer to ongoing problems of life, difficult emergencies, and governmental calamities.

Nothing-doing includes implicitly nothing-projecting. Compare nothing-projecting with such sayings as "take no thought for the morrow" and "there is no time but this present." [Matthew 6:34 KJV; Fox, Epistle 5]

49.

Good to the Not-good

The sage has no fixed heart.
He finds his heart
In the hundred families' hearts.
He is good to the good;
He is also good to the not-good.
For virtue is good.
He is faithful to the faithful;
He is also faithful to the unfaithful,
For virtue is faithful.

Living beneath heaven,
The sage deals shyly with beneath-heaven
And simplifies his heart.
The hundred families strain eyes and ears;
The sage acts the child to all of them.

Good to the not-good. Inward recognition of Truth and the participation in it of all men constitute the pivotal elements of prophetic religion. Men of good will like Confucius hold that unkindness should be repaid with justice; otherwise, how should kindness be repaid? Men of prophetic inwardness, uninterested in notions of repayment, know that all men are one. Martin Buber, as already noted, translates Leviticus 19:18 as "You shall love your neighbor as one like yourself." (See commentary to Chapter 22.) The Sermon on the Mount [Matthew 5:44*ff.*] links common sonship, love of enemies, and the Way of creation with divine impartiality:

> He makes his sun rise on the evil and the good,
> and sends rain on the just and the unjust.

The prophets sense that the closeness of God to man depends on the closeness of man to man; hence arise their testimonies against violence, oppression, and conspicuous living. In the Gospel of Luke [6, 27-28, 35], Jesus declares:

> Love your enemies, do good to those who hate you:
> bless those who curse you, pray for those who
>   abuse you....
> [Y]ou will be sons of the Most High—
> for he is kind even to the ungrateful and the evil.

George Fox was sufficiently imbued with this prophetic spirit to forget on occasion even to mention the not-good, as when he advised Friends "to walk cheerfully around the world answering that of God in every man," and when he stressed, in one of his many pamphlets, "Doing Truth to all, without respect to persons; to high and low whatsoever, young or old, rich or poor." [*Journal*, 1656, p. 263; Line of Righteousness, 1661]

One of the Hasidic teachers says, "The real love of God should begin with the love of man. And if anyone should tell you that he has love of God but has no love of man, then know that he is lying." [*Hasidism*, p. 168] According to the early Quakers, there is a divine light in every man. According to the early Hasidim, there is a divine particle in every man—and one, moreover, that is peculiar to him. Hence every man without exception, the righteous and the unrighteous, has divine worth. Yehiel Michal of Zlotchov says, "Pray for your enemies that all may be well with them. And should you think this is not serving God, rest assured that more than all prayers, this is, indeed, the service of God." [*Tales*, p. 156]

50.

Thirteen

Going out is life;
Coming back is death.
The companions of death are thirteen.
The companions of life are thirteen.
For people moving toward death
There are also thirteen.
How is that?
Because they overreach life.

It is said that
He who preserves his life
Meets no tigers or wild buffaloes on the road,
Remains untouched by weapons in the wars.
In him, the wild buffalo
Finds no space for his horns,
The tiger no space for his claws,
The soldier no space for his blade.
How is this?
Because there is no space for death in him.

The thirteen companions. It is not known what these were, and what has been suggested seems to add little sense to a paragraph lacking in it. *Thirteen* in this chapter reads literally *ten-have-three*. It can be held to mean *three of*

146

ten; so holds the Wang Pi commentary. *Ten-plus-three* is preferred by many commentators because of comparable usage elsewhere in the Tao Teh Ching, and because the sense of the chapter remains strained, unless the meaning is strained further by trying to guess the hidden etymological significance of ancient ideographs. Can it be that *three of ten* reflects the three-fold division of humanity into those who divide things in three, those who do not, and those who cannot? In this jocular view, a *three of ten* reading puts Lao Tzŭ in the *cannot* fold. No way can ten be divided by three without one left over.

No space for death. Notwithstanding the imagery of the second paragraph, Lao Tzŭ gives simple and repeated witness to immortality. (See Chapters 16 and 52.) This paragraph has the spirit, however, of later Taoism: corrupt not because of imagery, but because deathlessness is attributed not to Tao but to a human being who preserves his own life, possibly by magic. Or Lao Tzŭ, unknowing of what later would happen, was not sufficiently precise.

51.

Tao Gives Life

Tao gives them life;
Virtue nurses them;
Reality shapes them;
Chance completes them.
Thus the ten thousand things
All worship Tao and esteem virtue.
No one commands them
To worship Tao and esteem virtue.
They do so of themselves.

For Tao gives them life.
Virtue nurses them, raises them,
Nurses them, shelters them,
Comforts them, feeds them,
And protects them.

Rear but don't own!
Work but don't claim!
Raise but don't butcher!
This is called inward virtue.

Raise but don't butcher! If Tao does not butcher us who are Tao's children, why have we the effrontery to butcher those children of Tao who are also our children? Tao does not lead us to goodness by force or manipulation or deceit. Why then should we feel obliged to so lead our children, compelling them, tricking them, lying to them, with the excuse of trying to prod them into outward virtue? We do so, we tell ourselves, because we love our children. What worse could we do to persons we hate? Following the Way of nursing, sheltering, comforting, feeding, and protecting is, by contrast, useful, pleasing, and enjoyable. In the manner that the splendor of Tao informs and directs us, so may our more homey example inform and direct. We possess other people—including the children we think of as ours—no more than we possess ourselves, and what we neither possess nor are possessed by can best be left to Tao and its workings.

For the wonder of children, see Lao Tzŭ's experience of them in Chapter 55. For the delight of leaving them to the Way, along with everything else that presents serious and pressing problems, see the entire Tao Teh Ching.

52.

Keep to Weakness

Beneath-heaven has a beginning:
The mother of beneath-heaven.
Knowing the mother,
We may know the children.
Knowing the children,
We may keep to the mother.
Death of body? No risk!

> Block the passages,
> Shut the doors:
> End of life? No fuss!
> Open the passages,
> Meddle with things:
> End of life? No help!
>
> See the small: that is insight.
> Keep to weakness: that is strength.
> Use the light: go back to insight,
> Keeping away from calamity
> And practicing the changeless.

Blocked passages and *shut doors* are the beneficent consequence of openness to the mother which is Tao. They are not at all the same as non-attachment of the closed-in sort that refuses such openness. Affection and compassion are not evidences of attachment to pretensions and possessions, but of deliverances from them. Silence in the face of sorrow and joy is commonly taken to indicate Oriental impassivity, but is simply evidence of Western parochialism concerning divergent ways of life. Such mannerisms are often treated in Western literature as bizarre and bereft of human feeling.

53.

Robber-braggarts

> If I have a grain of wisdom,
> I walk along the great Tao
> And only fear to stray.
>
> The great Tao is easy indeed,
> But the people choose by-paths.
> The court is very resplendent;
> But very weedy are the fields
> And the granaries very empty.

They wear gaudy clothes,
Carry sharp swords,
Exceed in eating and drinking,
Have more riches than they can use.
Call them robber-braggarts:
They are anti-Tao indeed!

Robber-braggarts. "What mean you," demands Isaiah, "by crushing my people and grinding the face of the poor?" [Isaiah 3:15] He is anguished by the rich: "their land so full of silver and gold, no end to their stores, their land so full of horses, no end to their war-chariots." [Isaiah 3:15, 2:17] The same theme is found in the Gospels, and the Epistle of James [5:1-6] declares it again, to the embarrassment of some of the latter day rich.

Come now, you rich men, weep and shriek
   over your impending miseries!
You have been storing up treasure in the
   very last days;
your wealth lies rotting,
and your clothes are moth-eaten;
your gold and silver lie rusted over
and their rust will be evidence against you....
You have condemned, you have murdered
   the righteous—unresisting.

The last two lines of Chapter 53 pun seriously on the words *robbers* and *Tao*, which are pronounced the same. The gaudily clothed can thus be Tao-braggarts and, consequently, can be against Tao in their being as well as against Tao in their behavior.

54.

Inward Light!

What is well planted won't be uprooted;
What is well grasped won't slip away.
Sons and grandsons will keep the sacrifices.

Practice virtue in yourself:
Virtue becomes real.
Practice it in the family:
It becomes overflowing.
Practice it in the village:
It becomes lasting.
Practice it in the country:
It becomes prolific.
Practice it beneath heaven:
It becomes universal.

Thus persons are to be looked at
As a person,
Families as a family,
Villages as a village,
Countries as a country,
Beneath-heaven as beneath-heaven.
How do I know about beneath-heaven?
Inward Light!

Inward Light! The inwardness which Lao Tzŭ designates by the pronoun *this* is the Way by which we are taught as well as the Way upon which we journey. That is, men and women follow Light, and it is Light that informs them both about Truth and the road on which it is to be followed. "And this," said George Fox after an experience of inward opening, "I knew experimentally." [*Journal*, 1647] Prophetic individuals characteristically experience inward truths, of which Light is one, as incontrovertible facts of experience. The Psalmist [51:6] says:

'Tis inward truth that thou desirest;
grant me then wisdom in my secret heart.

The third line in the first paragraph on sacrifices is in consonance with a book of filial piety, but not with the Tao Teh Ching, which looks askance at sacrifices, at fealty, and at piety. Fealty to a landed overlord, which appeared

151

in China about the beginning of the Bronze Age, leads easily to duty and obligation to a family patriarch.

55.

Infant Vitality

One who is weighty in virtue
Resembles an infant child.
Poisonous insects don't sting him;
Wild beasts don't seize him;
Birds of prey don't strike him.
His bonds are soft,
His sinews tender,
Yet his grip is strong.
He does not know
The union of male and female,
Yet his virility is evident,
His vitality perfect.
He cries and howls all day,
But does not get hoarse.
Perfect harmony!

To know harmony
Is to know the changeless.
To know the changeless
Is to have insight.
It is ominous
To improve on life,
Violent to
Control breathing by the mind:
Things overgrown fall into decay.
This is not-Tao,
And what is not-Tao soon ends.

An infant child. Return to infancy! Jesus says, "I tell you truly, unless you turn and become like children, you will never get into the Realm of Heaven at all. Whoever humbles himself like this child, he is the greatest in the Realm of Heaven." [Matthew 18:3-4]

Dov Bear of Mezritch says, "From the child you can learn three things: He is merry for no particular purpose; Never for a moment is he idle; When he needs something, he demands it vigorously." [*Tales*, p. 105] While Calvin held that children were corrupt even before birth, infant sanctity characterized many other faiths.

His virility is evident and *His vitality perfect* are references to infant sexuality.

Control breathing. From this saying and from the comment on foreknowledge in Chapter 38, it may be assumed that practices associated with later Taoism and with the Buddhism later imported into China existed a long time, at least, before the times of Lao Tzŭ. That the early teaching of Tao had little impact on the prevalence of magic suggests that the latter-day practice of it had long roots. To Lao Tzŭ, of course, magic practices were uncongenial; popular indifference to his teachings about them is one sign of how truly unsuccessful he was.

56.

The Original Oneness

He who knows does not speak;
He who speaks does not know.

Block the passages!
Shut the doors,
Blunt edges,
Untie tangles,
Harmonize lights,
Unite all dust.
Call this the original oneness.
It can't be had by courting,
Can't be had by shunning;
Can't be had by helping,

Can't be had by harming;
Can't be had by praising,
Can't be had by blaming:
For it is beneath-heaven's highest.

Far above all antitheses is Tao, which makes ordinary opposites mean no more than the same thing: those very opposites by which human beings like to think they live, and over which they make much fuss. Praise and blame, as a Chinese adage has long held, are very much the same; indeed, they are functions of the same fixation on self that prevents turning to Tao, as do other fixations like helping and harming or other dodges like overreaching life and overdoing emotion. (Hence the need for blocking passages.) With this willfulness, the paradox of the first two lines may seem to have little connection, and yet reading and rereading the lines do reveal a connection, as happens with many passages in the Tao Teh Ching. He who speaks does not know: he substitutes personal eloquence for beyond-personal Truth.

57.

Law and Thieves

Govern the country by regular rules;
Direct the army by cunning moves;
But win the world by avoiding fuss.
How do I know that this is so?
Inward Light!

Beneath heaven
The more rules and prohibitions there are,
The poorer the people become.
The sharper the weapons are,
The greater the country's confusion.
The cleverer the people become,
The more cunning acts take place.

The more laws and orders there are,
The more thieves and robbers appear.

Therefore the sage says:
I do nothing,
And the people of themselves reform.
I love stillness,
And the people of themselves go straight.
I don't fuss,
And the people of themselves get rich.
I don't want,
And the people of themselves grow simple.

Win the world by avoiding fuss. About 1660, George Fox advised Quakers how Truth should be advanced in the world at large: "Let your conversation [demeanor] preach to all men and your innocent love.... Live in the peaceable life, doing good to all men, and seeking the good and welfare of all men." [Paper to Friends etc., Swarthmore Manuscripts 7:46] He also urged Friends to "walk cheerfully over the world answering that of God in every man." (See commentary to Chapter 49.)

Roughly a hundred years later, Israel of Rizhyn said, "If a man speaks in the spirit of truth and listens in the spirit of truth, one word is enough, for with one word can the world be uplifted, and with one word can the world be redeemed." [*Tales*, p. 236]

Martin Buber has written, "If we had power over the ends of the earth, it would not give us that fulfillment of existence which a quiet devoted relationship to nearby life can give us. If we knew the secrets of the upper worlds, they would not allow us so much actual participation in true existence as we can achieve by performing, with holy intent, a task belonging to our daily duties. Our treasure is hidden beneath the hearth of our own home." [*The Way of Man*, p. 30] What is done by being does more than what is done by doing—and by speaking. Being changes life; doing doesn't. And much noise does not accompany Truth.

58.

Simple Simple

When the law is dumb dumb,
The people are simple simple.
When the law is smart smart,
The people are broke broke.

Good fortune rests on bad fortune.
Bad fortune hides in good fortune.
Who knows the end of this?
It does not stop:
The normal turns into the odd;
The good turns into the weird.
Long have the people been in a stew!

Therefore the sage
Squares, but doesn't cut;
Exacts, but doesn't hurt;
Shapes, but doesn't strain;
Brightens, but doesn't dazzle.

Cleverness is the work of governments which choose to be smart instead of dumb. A short view of organized efforts on behalf of the people suggests that cleverness on behalf of the people usually perpetuates whatever hurts on the grounds that eradication of it would hurt more; thus laxity in banking must be preserved or the people will have no banks. Sometimes it appears that the clever way to rid the people of their troubles is to get rid of the people. To be clever is indeed to be weird. Much cleverness in equalizing taxes to improve employment, investment, and the well-being of all the people finds fruition in making the rich pay less and the poor pay more. Who would not prefer the dumbness of the sage, who does not strain or dazzle?

Long have the people been in a stew can be rendered less vulgarly as "Long have the people been astray."

59.

A Strong Stem

In ruling people and serving heaven,
It is best to be sparing.
To be sparing is to yield quickly.
To yield quickly is to double-store virtue.
If virtue is double-stored,
Nothing can't be overcome.
When nothing can't be overcome,
No one knows his limits.
When no one knows his limits,
That one can take on the country.
When that one takes on
The mother of the country,
He can last and endure.

Call this having deep roots
And a strong stem:
Living, lasting,
And seeing into Tao.

Chain argument. The entire progress of this chapter involves forging links from *being sparing* all the way up to *seeing into Tao.* The question is whether the links are philological rather than psychological in character: *i.e.,* whether they are arbitrary rather than realistic, and thus concerned with name-calling and the rectifying of terms, as are not a few early Chinese writings, including a number of the Confucian classics. In the Tao Teh Ching, chain argument is present also in chapters 16, 38, and 67.

Examination of each of the coupled links in the Tao Teh Ching suggests that they represent aspects of life as it is lived, not concepts about life as they can be juggled. Chain argument is not alone an early Chinese literary device. It is not uncommon among prophetic writings of a realistic character, including some of relatively recent appearance. In 1746, John Woolman wrote, "Doth pride lead to vanity? Doth vanity form imaginary wants? Do these wants prompt men to exert their power in requiring that of others which themselves would rather be excused from…? Do these proceedings beget hard thoughts? Do hard thoughts, when ripe, beget malice? Does malice, when ripe, become revengeful, and in the end inflict terrible pains on fellow creatures and spread desolations in the world?" [*Journal*, 1764]

60.

Cooking a Small Fish

Rule a big country
As you would cook a small fish.

When beneath-heaven is ruled with Tao,
Demons don't go spiriting.
Not only do the demons not spirit,
But the spirits don't harm people.
Not only do the spirits do no harm,
But the sage also does no harm.
Since both do no harm,
Virtue is restored intact.

Demons and *spirits*. It is as startling to come across, however briefly, aspects of superstition in the icono-clastic Tao Teh Ching as it would be to come across a favorable mention of idols in the Book of Isaiah. The only possible meaning that can be extracted from this chapter, as we have it, is one taken by conventional people: if the government is in order, discordant and irrational elements are thereby rendered ineffective, a notion that has Con-fucian roots but not early Taoist ones. It can be argued, of course, and perhaps correctly, that the text has been corrupted by various glosses and rewritings, but this argu-ment is of somewhat limited use in reading scriptures to find a Way, however great its use may be in exploring difficult areas of philology. For the moment one argues that troublesome passages are corruptions, one attributes a subjectivity to the text that clouds the whole of it with unreality.

To repeat, it may be better simply to sideline troublesome passages and let them stay inactive unless they become clear later on. It is useful to practice this trick when reading the Tao Teh Ching. Many Westerners could learn to use it in reading their own scriptures. Inherited notions of neatness, logical precision, and absence of contradiction present difficulties in understanding a Book so sacrosanct that any reference to it is usually capitalized.

Consciously or unconsciously, it is held that the Jewish and Christian Bibles and all of their parts are the final word of God and not his original inspiration. The insights of scripture are far too searching and meaningful to be blocked by artificial notions of tidiness. For an example of early Taoist insight, note the first two lines of Chapter 60, an insight of value particularly in places where food is systematically overcooked.

61.

Winning by Lowering

A great country is one that downward flows
To be a confluence of all beneath heaven
And beneath-heaven's female.
For the feminine overcomes the masculine
By quietude and lowliness.

Hence,
By lowering itself before a small country,
A great country wins over a small country.
By lowering itself before a large country,
A small country wins over a large country.
The one wins by lowering itself,
The other by keeping itself lowered.

159

Great countries wish nothing more
Than to shelter people;
Small countries wish nothing more
Than to have their people sheltered.
Since each gets its wish,
The great country ought to make itself lower.

Winning by lowering. By the sixth century B.C. in China, war and violence were no longer occasional outbreaks but continuing upheavals. The separate states that composed the Chou Empire fought regularly among themselves and against Chou, weakened after some five centuries of rule. To have expected any country participating in this ongoing strife suddenly to attempt victory by lowering itself would have been similar to expecting any of the nobles participating in the oppressions of the times to lower himself before the oppressed, who in those Bronze Age times were confined to a Neolithic manner of living.

Did Lao Tzŭ tell a tale of Tao that would apply only out of time, out of space, and finally out of this world? When Isaiah, in an environment of comparable violence and oppression, expressed his vision of a peaceable kingdom, was he too projecting a future outside of reality? For he said, "Nation shall not lift up sword against nation, neither shall they learn war any more." [Isaiah 2:4 KJV]

And what was Jesus projecting when he said, "Resist not evil?" [Matthew 5:39 KJV]

Ever since these teachings were uttered, the conventionally minded have sought to banish them from this life at least. They are, however, part of the Way, and that Way is not invalidated by the world's not having reached the destination of it. If human life continues despite violence, it will be because teachers such as Lao Tzŭ, Isaiah, and Jesus envisioned long ago the likelihood of men, women, and children realizing increasingly in historic time the evidences of the Way they come to know in their daily undertakings. It will be because teachings of the Way have not been banished from the hearts of common

ordinary men, including common ordinary conventional-
ists, for people who are inclined by mental habit to trust in
violence are notably out of touch with their own hearts.
The Realm of Truth, of God, of Tao comes into the world
only through inward existence of committed lives.

62.

Found if Sought

Tao is the refuge of the ten thousand things:
The treasure of the good man,
The backstop of the not-good man.
Fine words can be sold.
Noble deeds gain respect.
Even not-good people
Are not rejected.

When an emperor is enthroned
Or the three ministers installed,
Disks of jade and teams of horses
Are not as gifts the equal
Of sitting still and offering Tao.

Why did the ancients prize the Tao?
Because if it is sought, it is found;
Because the guilty are forgiven.
That is why it is beneath-heaven's treasure.

If it is sought, it is found. The Gospel of Matthew says: [in
the seventh verse of the seventh chapter]

Ask and the gift will be yours,
seek and you will find,
knock and the door will open to you....

Even not-good people / Are not rejected. These lines can be
translated to read *If a man is not good, / Why throw him*

161

away? This reading ties the chapter together by suggesting that fine words, noble things, and even not-good men are usable as gifts; therefore why not give the real treasure, Tao? Commentators have not generally followed such a reading, since it turns *a man's not-goodness* into *things men think not-good*, for which there does not seem to be textual warrant, and in the way of which stands a particle that can be treated as a sign of the possessive. This translation here follows Professor Henricks.

63.

Exalt the Low, Multiply the Few

Do nothing-doing;
Manage nothing-managing;
Taste nothing-tasting.
Exalt the low;
Multiply the few;
Repay hatred with virtue.

Tackle the difficult when it is easy.
Handle the big when it is small.
Difficult things beneath heaven
Are made up of easy things.
Big things beneath heaven
Are made up of small things.
Thus the sage
Never deals with the great,
But accomplishes greatness.

Light promises indeed lack trust.
Much easiness leads to much difficulty.
Thus the sage
Holds everything difficult,
But meets no difficulty in the end.

Lao Tzŭ's great do-nothing chapter is one of a series of writings in the Teh section of his book on the intensely practical advantages of opening up to Tao and of letting its power penetrate the problems and perplexities of personal, familial, commercial, governmental, and even historical relationships. Nothing-doing is the key to these practical advantages, and for all the paradoxicality of its presentation, intensely practical itself: practical because it is not conventional. It resembles psychologically those types of infighting, serious or sportive, whereby the opponent's thrust is used to throw him, and is part of a series of feints, dodges, and like ruses used to confuse and overcome those who are acquainted only with conventional overpowering force, and who are innocent of the vast arsenal of tricks that are used by seeming midgets to overcome apparent giants.

But the strategems are fruitful in human intercourse only if they are grounded in the tremendous, overwhelming, and ultimate reality of Tao. If they are grounded in self, the principal claimant against Tao, virtue itself fails. "When Tao is lost," reads Chapter 38, "there is virtue." High virtue is literally its own reward, for no social good comes of it. But low virtue, which serves private ends, is monstrous, as it was proposed to be by China's legalist school of thought and as proved to be by dictatorship in the brief Ch'in Dynasty (255-206 B.C.).

Repay hatred with virtue. It is to be recalled that Confucius, philosopher of ritual and order—when asked whether unkindness should be repaid with kindness— asked in reply how kindness then would be repaid, and said: "Repay unkindness with justice." [Analects 25:36]

64.

Dare Not Do

What is at rest is easy to hold.
What hasn't happened is easy to forestall.
What is brittle is easy to break.
What is minute is easy to scatter.

Deal with a thing before it exists;
Handle disorder before it takes place.

A tree of a full span's girth
Springs from a tiny sprout.
A nine-story tower
Rises from a clod of earth.
A journey of a thousand miles
Starts from where your feet are.

Whoever acts spoils;
Whoever grasps loses;
The sage does nothing;
Therefore he spoils nothing.
He grasps nothing;
Therefore he loses nothing.

People often spoil things
At the point of success.
Take it easy
At the finish as well as the start;
Then nothing will be spoiled.

Therefore the sage
Desires to be desireless,
Does not prize rare goods,
Learns to unlearn his learning,
Returns the people to what they have lost,
Helps all things find their nature,
But dares not do.

With Tao this chapter, composed largely of old Chinese
saws, is vital and compelling. Without Tao, it is dull and
obvious. To penetrate this and many other passages in the
Tao Teh Ching, keep first in mind Lao Tzǔ's words from
Chapter 19: "Reduce the self and curb desire." In sum, get
self out of the way of Tao and get out of the habit of
overreaching life, of looking to it for the excitements,

excesses and extravagances (whether of high ego or low ego) behind which self hides from Tao: the simple prophetic message that people for at least two and a half millenia have wanted to hear but have usually been loath to follow.

65.

Cleverness

The ancients well versed in Tao
Did not enlighten the people
But kept them simple-minded.

Why are the people hard to govern?
Because they are too clever.
Clever government is a curse,
Non-clever government a blessing.
To know these two things
Is to follow the ancient pattern,
And to know the ancient pattern
Is original virtue.

Original virtue is far-reaching and deep.
It leads all things to return
Back to the great harmony.

Did not enlighten the people. Enlightening them, Lao Tzŭ declares, would be a curse: a curse to them. It would lead back to enlightened and clever government. The Tao Teh Ching aims not to keep down the people but to liberate them: liberate them from the oppression that is a consequence of cleverness, from the violence that is a part of government that considers itself enlightened. Clever manipulators who want for the people no schools, poor dwellings, and little food are robber-braggarts who will find in Tao no place to hide. Cleverness is so far from the Way that, whether well- or ill-intentioned, it is a principal manifestation of not-goodness.

66.

Don't Compete!

Rivers and seas
Become kings of the hundred valleys
Because they lie lower.
That is why they become kings.

Hence the sage,
Wishing to be higher than the people,
Keeps his speech lower;
Wishing to lead the people,
Puts himself behind them.

For the sage
Stays above the people,
But they don't feel weight;
Stays in front,
But they don't feel hurt.

Thus, beneath-heaven
Gladly upholds him
And does not weary of him.

Because he does not compete,
Nobody beneath heaven
Can compete with him.

Puts himself behind them. It is recorded [Luke 18:16] that:

> everyone who uplifts himself will be humbled
> and he who humbles himself will be uplifted.

The world of overreaching competition hears the counsel of lowliness advanced by Lao Tzŭ and Jesus without opening ears to it, reads it while closing eyes to it. In that world the value of a human being is determined by how high he is above other human beings, and his lowness (unless it is worn as a badge) is a neurotic discomfort he

166

admits only when he can get high on it. Long have men and women been educated to get rid of their natural affections and to compete, to distinguish one from another on the basis of intellect, income, fashion, fad, health, illness, anything that lends itself to the disparagements of rank. Even as a competitive social epoch comes to an end, there is fresh competition, enlivened in the final days by conflict between one sex and another, between one age group and another, between one race or one people and another. Competition, like a sword, has been sharpened so relentlessly that it can no longer hold an edge.

67.

Unlikely

All beneath heaven say
My great Tao seems unlikely.
But it is great
Because it seems unlikely.
Were it not unlikely,
Long indeed would it have been petty.

I have three treasures,
Held close and guarded.
The first is love.
The second is simplicity.
The third is not-daring
To be first beneath heaven.
Whoever is loving can be brave;
Whoever is simple can be generous;
Whoever is not-daring
To be first beneath heaven
Can be a vessel of excellence.
But to be brave without being loving,
Generous without being simple,
Foremost without being hindmost,
This is to perish!

For:
Love cannot fight without winning,
Cannot defend without strengthening.
When heaven helps
It protects by loving.

Translated as love is a character that also means mercy or pity or compassion. The type of love here referred to resembles agape and is of a tender and maternal nature. Lao Tzǔ holds firmly to the distaff side.

The first paragraph is here translated to mean that great Tao is, in the world's terms, unlikely. Another possible translation is that the world terms Tao great but unlikely, but such translation seems to complicate rather than clarify. *Unlikely* is sometimes translated as *folly*, a more incisive word, but one that seems to over-stretch the sense of the original character.

68.

Non-competing

A good soldier is not violent;
A good fighter has no wrath.
The best way to win over an enemy
Is not to compete with him.
The best way to use a man
Is to work under him.
Call this not-competing in virtue.
Call this using human strengths.
Call this mating with heaven as of old!

Work under. The saying of Jesus [Matthew 23:11] is one of his teachings of the last interchanging with the first:

He who is greatest among you must be your servant.
Whoever uplifts himself will be humbled,
and whoever humbles himself will be uplifted.

Speechwriters for conservative dignitaries have tried to stretch the teachings of Lao Tzŭ into a defense of what is called a free market. These speechwriters, and by extension their dignitaries (modern clones of the ancient legalists) misunderstand Tao when they use it as a screen to justify personal greed freed from social restraints. The Tao Teh Ching, among other things, is a polemic against greed and against dignitaries. It is, at the same time, a polemic against rigid concepts and confining projections. Things are not to be thought out ahead but dealt with as they occur, and decisions are to be made not from confining concepts and logical projections but from the nature and creative flow of events as they take place.

69.

Marching by Not-marching

The strategists have a saying:
I dare not be a host,
But rather a guest;
Dare not advance an inch,
But rather retreat a foot.
This is called
Marching by not marching,
Capturing by not baring arms,
Charging by not attacking,
Holding by not bearing arms.

There is no evil heavier
Than to make light of an enemy.
To make light of an enemy
Is to lose what we value.
Thus when armies clash,
The one that grieves wins.

Holding by not bearing arms. The book of Isaiah [9:9-10] describes the sad alternative to the Peaceable Kingdom:

Arm for the fray,
and you will be shattered!…
Form your plot,
and it will fail.

Abraham the Angel (d.1776) says, "I have learned a new
form of service from the wars of Frederick, King of
Prussia. It is not necessary to approach the enemy in order
to attack him. In fleeing from him, it is possible to
circumvent him as he advances, and fall on him from the
rear until he is forced to surrender. What is needed is not
to strike straight at Evil, but to withdraw to the sources of
divine power, and from there to circle around Evil, bend it
and transform it into its opposite." [*Tales*, p. 115] This
statement is a meaningful commentary on overcoming evil
by not resisting it, but it is also a reasonably exact description of Chinese guerrilla tactics, hinted at in the Tao
Teh Ching, defined by the strategist Sun Tzŭ, described in
numerous Chinese novels, and practiced by Chinese
armies as late as the Second Battle of Changsha, the first
and now-forgotten allied victory in the second World War,
which was won by Taoist-like indirection.

The first five lines of this chapter follow Dr. Wu.

70.

Jade Inside Himself

My words are very easy to know,
Very easy to follow;
But beneath-heaven can't know them,
Can't follow them.

My deeds have an ancestor;
My deeds have a lord.
People don't know him,
So they don't know me.
The fewer who know me,
The more honored I am.

170

> The sage wears coarse clothing,
> Inside himself hides jade.

Unpopular is the role of prophet. John Woolman says, "The messages of the prophet Jeremiah were so disagreeable to the people, and so reverse to the spirit they lived in, that he became the object of their reproach, and in the weakness of nature thought to desist from his prophetic office; but, said he, *His word was in my heart as a burning fire shut up in my bones*, and I was weary with forbearing and could not stay. I saw at this time that if I was honest to declare that which Truth opened in me, I could not please all men.... From one age to another, the gloom grows thicker and darker, till error gets established by general opinion, so that whoever attends to perfect goodness and remains under the melting influence of it, finds a path unknown to many and sees the necessity to lean upon the arm of divine strength and dwell alone or with a few in the right." [*Journal*, 1756, 1759] Prophets are in the position of overturning convention in order to turn conventional people right side up. But conventional people turn the prophets out.

71.

Sick of Sickness

> To know and to be unknowing is best;
> Not to know and to be knowing is sickness.
> Only by being sick of our sickness
> Are we not sick.
>
> The sage is not sick.
> He is sick of his sickness
> And therefore not sick.

The first two lines of this chapter are among the most difficult in the Tao Teh Ching to translate. Literally,

they read: "Know not know best. / Not know know sickness." All translators come up with different renderings,
and the reader is invited to come up with his own, bearing
in mind that words will have to be added and that verbs
can interchange with nouns. Some translators treat the first
two instances of *know* as nouns, whence comes the
following rendering: "To treat knowledge as ignorance is
best. / To treat ignorance as knowledge is sickness." The
present translation treats these two instances as verbal
forms and tries to be terse.

One of the two Mawangtui texts can, by the presence of
a ditto mark, be read as "Not know not know sickness," an
attractive solution to the problems of the chapter's first
two lines, which could then read, "To know that you don't
know is best; / Not to know that you don't know is sickness." But the ditto mark appears in no other text.

72.

No Show of Self

> When people don't fear force,
> Greater force then comes upon them.
> Don't meddle with their homes
> Or weary them at their work.
> Only when they are not wearied
> Will they not weary you.
>
> Therefore,
> The sage knows himself,
> But makes no show of himself.
> Loves himself,
> But does not exalt himself.
> He rejects the outward,
> Accepts the inward.

Does not exalt himself. John Woolman writes, "As death
comes to our own wills and a new way of life is formed in

us, the heart is purified and prepared to understand clearly...." [*Journal*, 1772] "When I silently ponder on that change that was wrought in me, I find no language equal to it, nor any means to convey to another a clear idea of it. I looked upon the works of God in this visible creation, and an awfulness covered me. My heart was tender and very often contrite, and a universal love in my fellow creatures increased in me. This will be understood by such who have trodden in the same path." [*Journal*, 1760]

The first five lines of the second paragraph of Chapter 72 come from Dr. Wu's translation, which concludes, "He prefers what is within to what is without." Terseness in the concluding two lines (which read literally *rejects that, accepts this*) is the aim of this translation.

73.

Attract without Summoning

The brave in daring die;
The brave in not-daring live.
Of these two,
One helps, the other hurts.
Heaven may hate,
But who knows why?
This question stumps the sage.

It is the Tao of heaven
To conquer without competing,
To answer without speaking,
To attract without summoning,
To plan without hastening.
Vast is heaven's net
And wide-meshed,
Yet nothing slips through.

The first of these two paragraphs is out of sorts not only with the second but also within itself. The brave in daring do die, and the brave in not-daring do live. But what connection does this suitably Taoist aphorism have with heaven hating and no one, not even the sage, knowing why? Conceivably the sense of these lines may turn on Heaven's having a corner on hatred (as it is said to have on vengeance) and on the consequent need for all others, including the sage, to back off from it. But, conceivably, there is no such sense at all in these lines, and possibly not any other sense. By contrast, the second paragraph shows a sense-making way to rule a country, run a business, or live with a spouse.

74.

Handling the Hatchet

When people don't mind death,
Why threaten them with death?
If, afraid of death,
They were still unruly,
Who would dare to seize and kill them?

The great executioner
Kills those who kill.
To take his place is like
Handling the hatchet
For a master carpenter.
Whoever handles the hatchet
For a master carpenter
Usually get his hands cut.

Afraid of death. Since Lao Tzŭ sees no trouble in death, why should he, in this chapter, write as if fear of death were something natural to the people of which the better-off had deprived them? Possibly, Lao Tzŭ was writing about that fear which is awe, but it is unwise to penetrate the text of this chapter by the use of surmise.

The great executioner. The word great is not in the

text, but it is approved by commentators and translators. *Master carpenter*, however, is great carpenter.

75.

Why People Starve

When people are starving,
Their rulers are taxing them heavily.
That is why they are starving.
When people are hard to govern,
Their rulers are something-doing.
That is why they are hard to govern.
When people make light of death,
Their rulers make much of life.
That is why they make light of death.

But not interfering with life
Is worthier than overreaching life.

Taxing and *something-doing*. The prophets of Israel see the sundering of man's oneness with the Most High in man's sundering his oneness with his fellow man, and they vehemently decry oppression in all forms. The very word jeremiad derives from the prophet Jeremiah's rolling denunciations, and Isaiah [10:1-3] declares:

Woe to those who issue harsh decrees,
    penning orders that oppress,
robbing the weak of their rights,
    and defrauding the poor of their dues,
till widows fall to them as spoil
    and orphans as their prey.
What will you do at the great Assizes,
    when the storm blows from abroad?

Jesus cries out, "Woe to you rich folk." [Luke 6:24] John Woolman, loving in manner and usually gentle in tone, writes, "And here luxury and covetousness, with all the numerous oppressions and other evils attending them, appeared very afflicting to me; and I felt in that which is immutable the seeds of great calamity and desolation are sown and growing on this continent." [*Journal*, 1763] "Thus oppression in the extreme appears terrible, but oppression in more refined appearances remains to be oppression; and where the smallest degree of it is cherished, it grows stronger and more extensive...." [*A Plea for the Poor*, 1793] He questions first himself: "Do I, in all my proceedings, keep to that use of things which is agreeable to universal righteousness?" [*Journal*, 1761]

76.

The Soft and Weak

A man lives soft and weak,
Dies hard and stiff.
The grass, the trees,
The ten thousand things
Live soft and supple,
Die brittle and dry.

Hence
The hard and stiff
Are followers of death;
The soft and weak
Are followers of life.

For
When armies are stiff,
They will lose;
When trees are stiff,
They will fall.
The stiff and mighty
Will be cast down;
The soft and weak
Will be lifted up.

The weak. The Psalmist [72:12-14] declares that, in the mind of Truth, though not the world, the weak fare well:

> For the Eternal saves the forlorn
>   who cry to him,
> the weak and the helpless;
> he pities the forlorn and weak,
> he saves the life of the weak,
> rescuing them from outrage
>   and oppression....

Mindful of the extortions and oppressions of the well-off, the Psalmist states further, "Happy is he who remembers the weak and the poor." [41:1]

77.

The Stretched Bow

Heaven's Tao is like a stretched bow:
The top goes down
And the bottom goes up.
What has much is shortened;
What has little is increased.

Heaven's Tao takes from those with much
And gives to those with little.
Man's way is not so:
It takes from those with little
And gives to those with much.

Who uses muchness
To serve beneath-heaven?
Only he who has Tao!
Therefore the sage
Does but does not claim,
Completes but takes no credit.
He does not want his merit seen.

To turn to Lao Tzŭ for information—philosophical, psychological, or social—is to read words seemingly of much the same purport and eventually to tire of the repetitive. Chapter 77, despite the fresh imagery of the stretched bow, indeed says what has been said before: that oppression comes not from Tao but from man, that wealth taken from the poor is not well used by those who follow wealth but only by those who follow Tao, and that the sage takes no credit and only seeks to hide. But the Tao Teh Ching is not a work of information, not a manual of ideas, concepts, philosophy or systematized religious reasoning. Perhaps it can be described as an outburst, an inspired breaking forth concerning reality: reality deep, broad, and high, natural reality, the reality of everything and of nothing in creation and beyond it.

The book is not to be studied but to be absorbed, to be read, read, read, and then to be reread and reread, for it is in the course of continuing exposure that the Way begins to dawn on the reader of it. Then repetition does not repeat, and successive readings prompt fresh reaction. The more Tao is read, the more intimate it becomes. But the more it is read, the less familiar it becomes also, for it becomes fresher with every exposure to it.

78.

Water

Nothing beneath heaven
Is softer and weaker than water.
Nothing is better
To attack the hard and strong,
And nothing can take its place.
The weak overcome the strong;
The soft overcome the hard.

There is no one beneath heaven
Who doesn't know this,
And no one who practices it.

Therefore the sage says:
To bear the dirt of the country
Is to be master of the grain-shrines.
To bear the sins of the country
Is to be the lord of beneath-heaven.
Indeed, straight words seem crooked!

It may be argued that the weak overcoming the strong and the bearer of a country's sins becoming the master of its granaries is not reality but whimsy, and that mastery belongs not to the weak who are underneath things but to the strong who are on top of them. This argument prevails in the West in times of prosperity. But it collapses upon exposure to the Way. For Tao is the Way, the Way in which heaven and beneath-heaven, all life and all creation are patterned to work.

79.

Lay No Guilt

When great ill-will is reconciled,
And there remains ill-will,
How shall it be made good?

By the sage holding the left-hand tally
And laying no guilt on others.
If you have virtue, you keep to the tally;
If you don't have virtue, you pyramid claims.
The Tao of heaven plays no favorites,
But it always succors the good.

The left-hand tally recorded debits, the right-hand tally credits. About the left-handed general, see Chapter 31. In effect, the sage holds to his word but does not force greedy opponents to hold to theirs. The Way, to repeat, is so patterned that this form of nothing-doing yields beneficent social results.

80.

A Small Country with Few People

Oh for a small country with few people!
There may be contrivances
Of ten-fold or hundred-fold productivity,
But the people don't use them.
Let the people mind death
And not move away.
Though there are boats and carriages,
There is no occasion to ride them.
Though there are weapons and arms,
There is no occasion to show them.
Let the people again knot cords.
Let them enjoy their food,
Take pleasure in their houses,
And delight in their customs.

Another country may be so near
That each hears the noise
Of the other's cocks and dogs,
But until the end of their days,
The two people never mingle.

Oh for a small country with few people, but we now live
in very large countries with many people, and in a world
that has suddenly become unimaginably populated, not
simply in terms of the Bronze Age but all of the centuries
preceding the current age of high technology. The vision of
a small country, attractive in its outward simplicity, was
one tenable in the Bronze Age, when it was still possible
to witness Neolithic simplifications with one's own eyes,
when the invention of bronze meant nothing better than
the production of sacrificial vessels (sometimes associated
with human sacrifice) and of cheaper and more destructive
weapons of war, when the invention of writing meant
nothing better than divination and the more exact
recording of taxes.

It is a vision that has been shared by some moderns of prophetic temper, such as Thoreau and Gandhi. Persons like John Woolman have also noted that the more anyone had, the less there was for everyone else to have, but this relationship pertained to pre-industrial economies based on scarcity and limited production. The dream of visible smallness and of visually obvious human interdependence is one whose inward reality could be felt only in less populated times. Be it remembered that Lao Tzŭ did not knot cords (the method of reckoning before the invention of writing); he wrote. What he wrote, indeed, was one of the early works that redeem a device originally given over to oppression and superstition. His vision of rustic isolation was a return to reality when he wrote about it, but today it is no longer a return but a backward look. A return to Tao is not a going backward.

Now any vision of isolation is gone. Were there to be substantially less machinery, transportation, and technology in the world, billions of people would, in effect, be sentenced to die. To some social reformers, including some who have wished to deprive poor countries of insecticides so that they would free themselves of the guilt of their rich countries making them, this eventuality seems not to be of primary concern, but it must be primary to any one who senses the oneness of mankind. Men and women are not created in such a way that they can seek spiritual reality in their own lives while looking upon, let alone condoning, the physical wasting and destruction of multitudes of their fellows. The reality behind Lao Tzŭ's vision can now be realized only in a world of many people, and that world continues to be a world of reality in which the Way loses no vigor.

Such a world is only slightly different, after all, from a world of a few people. The book of Tao is pertinent to both. It is possible to be simple in any circumstances, simplicity being the inward direction Lao Tzŭ described; and it may be that the more trying circumstances are, the easier it is to become simple.

81.

To Work but Not Compete

True words are not nice;
Nice words are not true.
A good man does not argue;
An arguer is not good.
The wise are not learned;
The learned are not wise.

The sage does not hoard.
The more he does for others,
The more he has himself.
The more he gives,
The more he gets.

The Way of Heaven is
To benefit but not to harm.
The Way of the sage is
To work but not compete.

Lao Tzŭ's final counsel is to keep away from niceness, to keep out of arguments, and to keep with simple factuality instead of cogitation's complex constructions: a useful counsel not only for making the most of life but also for finding the most in scripture. Upon finishing the reading of an unfamiliar scripture, the reader of modern habit finds it tempting to evaluate it, and thus to establish control over it by the processes of the intellect: a procedure not very different from some forms of stone-age superstition. Appreciate life, don't evaluate it; appreciate scripture, don't evaluate it. If it is worth reading, it is clearly beyond the evaluation of anyone, including the people who wrote it.

Comparisons will indeed come to mind. For example, Lao Tzŭ may not seem to be as vehemently dialogical as the prophets of Israel. But comparisons should not be kept in mind. The Tao Teh Ching is differently dialogical, but who is to say whether or not in itself it is equally or not equally dialogical? It is, among many other things, one of the most remarkable prayers ever uttered; to this prayer the whole Tao of creation gives dialogical answer.

The Tao Teh Ching, like other scriptures, has been readily misunderstood; the misunderstanding, and the tampering that results from attempts at understanding, are two of the reasons for its full translation in this volume. Before they were writ in stone, carved in wood, or printed repetitively on paper, early scriptures were subject to editing in terms of current times. Even latter-day scriptures have been subject to miscomprehension. The Word is greater than the words that describe it because it remains inalterable and all but unutterable.

True prophetic religions by their inward nature are not exclusive; they are supplemental. One scripture adds to the other, because one does not take the place of the other. Their similarities point to their common source, and the fact that they are so remarkably alike persuades not alone of their common but also of their particular truth. Particular truth, moreover, is the only way there is to common truth. All beings indeed have Tao in common, but there is no generalized Tao to which men and women can turn. For all its immediacy within us and around us, Tao is so wordlessly vast and so seemingly present that it is possible to find it only in the Tao that is particular to this one faith or that different faith, even though faith remains everywhere the same. When new faith supplements old faith, it renews. But when new faith supplants old faith, it deadens. It is unproductive to look at a new scripture as if it were something for which to give up the scripture one has. It is nourishing to add the new to the old.

William Penn writes: "The humble, meek, merciful, just, pious and devout souls are everywhere of one religion; and when death has taken off the mask, they will know one another, though the divers liveries they wear here make them strangers." [*Some Fruits of Solitude*, 1693, I: p. 519]

The Tao Virtue Classic
The Tao Teh Ching

1.

If Tao can be Taoed, it's not Tao.
If its name can be named, it's not its name.
Has no name: precedes heaven and earth;
Has a name: mother of the ten thousand things.

For it is
Always dispassionate:
See its inwardness;
Always passionate:
See its outwardness.

The names are different
But the source the same.
Call the sameness mystery:
Mystery of mystery, the door to inwardness.

2.

When all beneath heaven
Know beauty as beauty,
There is not beauty.
When all know good as good,
There is not good.

For what is and what is not beget each other;
Difficult and easy complete each other;
Long and short show each other;

High and low place each other;
Noise and sound harmonize each other;
Before and behind follow each other.

Therefore the sage
Manages without doing,
Teaches without talking.
He does not shun
The ten thousand things:
Rears them without owning them,
Works for them without claiming them,
Accomplishes but takes no credit.

Because he does not take credit,
It cannot be taken from him.

3.

If you don't exalt the worthy:
People then will not compete.
If you don't prize rare goods:
People then will not steal.
If you don't show what is covetable:
The people's hearts won't be upset.

Thus, when the sage rules,
He empties hearts
And fills bellies,
Weakens ambitions
And strengthens bones.
He leads the people
To not-know and not-want,
And the cunning ones
To dare not do.
By doing nothing-doing,
Everything gets done.

4.

Tao is empty! Use it
And it isn't used up.
Deep! It seems like
The forebear of
The ten thousand things.
It blunts edges,
Unties tangles,
Harmonizes lights,
Unites all dusts.

Submerged and existent!
I don't know whose child it is.
It looks to be the source.

5.

Heaven-and-earth is not humane:
It treats the ten thousand things
Like straw dogs.
The sage is not humane:
He treats the hundred families
Like straw dogs.

Heaven-and-earth and all between
Is like a bellows:
Empty but never used up.
The more it moves,
The more comes out of it.

Many words exhaust sense.
Keep to the empty center!

6.

The spirit of low places does not die.
Call its mysteriousness feminine.
The gate of this mysteriousness
Is the source of heaven-and-earth.
Unceasingly, unceasingly it seems to persist.
Use it and it won't wear out.

7.

Heaven abides; earth lasts.
They last and abide
By not living for themselves.
Hence they live forever.

Therefore the sage
Puts himself last,
Finds himself first;
Abandons his self,
Preserves his self.
Is it not because he has no self
That he is able to realize himself?

8.

True goodness is like water;
Water benefits the ten thousand things
But does not compete with them.
It stays in places disliked by man,
Therefore comes close to Tao.

For a dwelling keep to the ground.
In your heart keep to the deeps.

In dealing with others, keep to gentleness.
In speaking, keep to truth.
In governing, keep to order.
In business, keep to efficiency.
In making moves, keep the right pace.
If you do not compete,
You will not be faulted.

9.

Hold onto fullness?
It's better to stop.
Handle sharp edges?
They can't long be kept.
When gold and jade fill a house,
No one can protect it.
Pride in wealth and fame
Breeds its own collapse.

Do your work, retire:
This is the Tao of heaven.

10.

In maintaining the vital spirit,
Can you hold to oneness
And not come apart?

In developing the vital senses,
Can you be like an infant child?
In clearing the inward vision,
Can you be without guilt?
In loving the people and ruling the state,
Can you hold to nothing-knowing?
In opening and closing heaven's gate,

Can you act like a mother bird?
While seeing clearly in the four directions,
Can you hold to nothing-doing?

Rear the people,
Feed the people.
Rear them but don't own them.
Work but don't claim;
Lead but don't butcher.
Call this inward virtue.

11.

Thirty spokes share one hub;
In emptiness lies the wheel's utility.
Kneading clay makes a pot;
In emptiness lies the pot's utility.
Cutting doors and windows makes a room.
In emptiness lies the room's utility.

Gain can be had from somethingness,
But use can be had from nothingness.

12.

The five colors blind the eye.
The five notes deafen the ear.
The five flavors dull the taste.
Racing and hunting madden the heart.
Rare goods make men falter.

Therefore the sage
Tends the belly not the eye.
He rejects the outward,
Clasps the inward.

13.

Favor and disgrace: same fear.
Honor and distress: same self.

What is meant by:
"Favor and disgrace: same fear"?
Favor makes the lowly
Fearful when they get it,
Fearful when they lose it.
That's why favor and disgrace
Are the same fear.

What is meant by:
"Honor and distress: same self"?
The self registers our distress:
If we have no self,
We have no distress.

Therefore,
He who values all things as his self
Can manage all things.
He who loves all things as his self
Can be trusted with all things.

14.

Look at it; you can't see it:
Call it shadowless.
Listen to it; you can't hear it:
Call it soundless.
Grasp at it; you can't hold it:
Call it bodiless.

These three are beyond scrutiny;
Thus they merge into one.

Its upper side is not bright,
Its lower side not dark.
Continually the can't-be-named goes on
And comes back to nothingness.
Call it the formless form,
The imageless image,
The obscure.

From in front, you don't see its head.
From behind, you don't see its back.
But hold onto the Tao of old
And you can handle today's nowness.
Knowing the primal is the key to Tao.

15.

Tao's ancient masters were
Inwardly subtle and darkly perceptive.
Their depth was beyond understanding.

Because they were beyond understanding,
They can be described only by appearance:
Hesitant as if wading a river in winter,
Reluctant as if fearing a neighbor,
Reserved as if acting as guest,
Effacing like ice starting to melt,
Simple like uncarved wood,
Open like a valley,
Confused like muddy water.

Who else could clear muddy water
By quieting it?
Who else could move clear water
By bringing it to life?

Whoever keeps to Tao
Does not want to be full.

Not full, he can practice
Concealment instead of accomplishment.

16.

Reach utmost emptiness;
Hold fast to stillness.
The ten thousand things stir about;
I only watch for their going back.
Things flourish,
But each returns to its root.
Returning to the root is peace,
And peace is a going back to reality.

To go back to reality is to be constant;
To know the constant is to find insight;
Not to know the constant is to court calamity.

To know the constant is to be broad;
To be broad is to be just.
To be just is to be universal;
To be universal is to be heavenly.
To be heavenly is to find Tao;
To find Tao is to live forever
And to rob danger from death.

17.

Of the best ruler,
The people only know that he exists.
Next comes one they love and praise.
Next comes one they fear.
Next comes one they abhor.
When you are lacking in trust,

Others have no trust in you.
Of the work of one
Who is short with his words,
The hundred families say:
We have done it ourselves.

18.

When Tao is cast aside,
Duty and humanity abide.
When prudence and wit appear,
Great hypocrites are here.

When the six relations have no point,
Filial piety and paternal love are taught.
When the countryside is out of joint,
Loyal officials are man's lot.

19.

Give up wisdom,
Abandon knowledge,
And the people will
Benefit a hundredfold.
Give up benevolence,
Abandon righteousness,
And the people will
Go back to natural affection.
Give up cunning,
Abandon gain,
And robbers and thieves
Will disappear.

External rules are not enough;
Hold to what can be counted on:

Keep to simplicity,
Grasp the primal,
Reduce the self,
And curb desire.

20.

Give up learning:
Have no anxieties.
How much difference is there
Between ah and oh?
How much difference is there
Between good and evil?
What men fear
Must I fear?
Utter nonsense!

All men are happy happy,
As if consuming sacrificial feasts,
As if mounting the Spring Terrace.
I alone am mild,
Like one who gives no sign,
Like an infant who does not smile,
Forlorn, forlorn,
Like one with no place to go.

All men have plenty;
I alone am a loser,
A fool at heart indeed!
And stupid stupid!
The world's people are bright bright;
I alone am dull dull.
The world's people are smart smart;
I alone am low low,
Bland as the sea,
Aimless as the wind.

All men have their uses;
I alone am stubborn and uncouth.
But I differ most from the others
In prizing food drawn from my Mother.

21.

The nature of great virtue
Is to follow Tao alone.
And Tao's style is elusive, evasive.
Evasive, elusive,
Yet within it is form.
Elusive, evasive,
Yet within it is substance,
Dark and dim,
Yet within it is vitality.
Its vitality is very real:
Within it is trust.

From of old
Its name has not ceased,
For it has watched all beginnings.
How can all beginnings be watched?
Inward Light!

22.

Twist and get whole.
Bend and get straight.
Be empty and get filled.
Be worn and get renewed.
Have little: get much.
Have much: get baffled.

Therefore the sage
Holds to the One and
Becomes beneath-heaven's pattern.
He does not show himself,
Hence he shines;
Does not assert himself,
Hence he is seen;
Does not boast his merits,
Hence he gets credit;
Does not vaunt himself,
Hence he survives;
Does not compete with anyone,
Hence no one beneath heaven
Can compete with him.

The old saying,
The twisted shall be made whole,
Is no empty phrase.
Be whole and you will return.

23.

Nature speaks little.
Squalls do not last the morning
Nor downpours the day.
What stirs them up?
Heaven-and-earth!
Even heaven-and-earth
Does not long make a fuss.
How much less should men!

Therefore,
He who follows Tao
Is one with Tao.
He who follows virtue
Is one with virtue.

He who follows loss
Is one with his losses.
Virtue is glad to get
Whatever comes to virtue.
Loss is glad to get
Whatever comes to loss.

When you are lacking in trust,
Others will have no trust in you.

24.

On tiptoe you don't stand.
Astride you don't walk.
Showing yourself, you don't shine.
Asserting yourself, you don't show.
Boasting yourself won't get you credit.
Vaunting yourself won't let you endure.

In Tao, these things are called
Tumors and dregs, which all things abhor.
Whoever has Tao does not dwell on them.

25.

Something there is
Without form and complete,
Born before heaven and earth,
Solitary and vast,
Standing alone without change.
Everywhere pervading all things,
Mothering all beneath heaven.
I don't know its name;

I style it Tao,
And for want of a name call it great.
To be great is to go on.
To go on is to be far.
To be far is to return.

Therefore,
Tao is great.
Heaven is great.
Earth is great.
Man also is great.
The universe has four greats,
And man is one of them.

Man follows earth;
Earth follows heaven;
Heaven follows Tao;
Tao follows itself.

26.

The heavy is the root of the light.
The still is the master of the restless.

Therefore,
The sage travels all day,
But never leaves the baggage wagon.
Though there are arresting sights,
He does not stir but sits.

Why does the master
Of ten thousand chariots
Show levity to all beneath heaven?
Levity will uproot him,
Restlessness unman him.

27.

Good walkers leave no marks to track;
Good speakers leave no nits to pick.
Good reckoners use no computers.
Good lockers turn no keys,
Yet no one opens their locks.
Good binders tie no ropes,
Yet no one undoes their knots.

What is more,
The sage is always good at saving people:
No one is cast out.
He is also good at saving things:
No thing is cast out.
Call this following the light.

Hence good men teach the not-good.
Not-good men are the lessons of the good.
Not to esteem the teacher,
Not to love the lesson,
Is to go astray despite great learning.
Call this the subtle secret.

28.

Know the masculine;
Keep to the feminine.
Be beneath-heaven's ravine.
To be beneath-heaven's ravine
Is to stay with unceasing virtue
And to return to infancy.

Know the white;
Keep to the black.
Be beneath-heaven's model.

To be beneath-heaven's model
Is to stay with unerring virtue
And return to the limitless.

Know the glorious;
Keep to disgrace.
Be beneath-heaven's valley.
To be beneath-heaven's valley
Is to stay with constant virtue
And return again to simplicity.

When simplicity diversifies
It produces instruments
That the sage uses as officers.
Indeed, a great leader
Does little cutting.

29.

Does anyone want to take the world
And act on it?
I don't see how he can succeed.
The world is a sacred vessel
Not to be acted on.
Whoever acts on it spoils it;
Whoever grasps at it loses it.

Indeed, there is a time
For some things to go forward,
And some to go behind;
Some to blow hot,
And some to blow cold;
Some to grow in strength,
And some to decay;
Some to be up,
And some to be down.

Therefore the sage eschews
Excesses, extremes, and extravagances.

30.

He who uses Tao to guide rulers
Does not force beneath-heaven with arms.
Such things recoil on their users.

Where armies are
Briars and brambles grow.
Bad harvests follow big wars.
Be firm and that is all:
Dare not rely on force.
Be firm but not haughty,
Firm but not boastful,
Firm but not proud,
Firm when necessary,
Firm but non-violent.

Things that flourish
Fall into decay.
This is not-Tao,
And what is not-Tao
Soon ends.

31.

Fine weapons are tools of ill fortune;
All things seem to hate them.
Whoever has Tao does not depend on them.

At home a gentleman favors the left;
In war he favors the right.

Since weapons are tools of ill fortune,
They are not tools for a gentleman,
Who uses them only from necessity.
Peace and quiet he upholds;
Victory he does not enjoy.
To enjoy victory is to like slaughter.
Whoever likes it
Cannot thrive beneath heaven.

Things of good omen favor the left:
Things of ill omen favor the right.
The under-general stands to the left;
The top-general stands to the right:
The way to stand at a burial rite.
Killing multitudes brings weeping and sorrow;
Treat victory like a funeral.

32.

Tao is always without name,
Simple and small.
Beneath-heaven dares not subject it.
If kings and barons can hold to it,
The ten thousand things will pay homage.
Heaven and earth will mutually join,
And sweet dew will fall.
Not by law but of themselves
The people will stay in balance.

When law and order arose,
Names appeared.
Aren't there enough already?
Is it not time to stop?
To know when to stop
Is to be free from danger.

Tao is to all beneath heaven
As rivers and seas are to
Rivulets and streams.

33.

Whoever knows others has wisdom;
Whoever knows himself has insight.
Whoever conquers others has force;
Whoever conquers himself has strength.
Whoever knows he has enough has wealth.
Whoever perseveres has purpose.
Whoever keeps to one place endures.
Whoever dies without perishing lives long.

34.

The great Tao flows everywhere:
It can go to the right or the left.
The ten thousand things draw life from it,
And it does not deny them.

It completes its work
But takes no title.
It clothes and feeds the ten thousand things
But does not own them.
You can call it small.
The ten thousand things return to it,
But it does not own them.
You can call it great.

Because it does not seek to be great,
Its greatness is accomplished.

35.

Hold to the great symbol:
All beneath heaven will follow,
Follow without harm,
Quiet, even, secure.

Music and dainties
Make passing guests pause.
But Tao is bland and without taste.
Looked at, it can't be seen;
Listened to, it can't be heard;
Used, it can't be used up.

36.

What is going to shrink has first been stretched.
What is going to weaken has first been made strong.
What is going to be ruined has first been raised up.
What is going to be taken away has first been given.
Call this the subtle truth:
The soft and weak conquer the hard and strong.

Fish should not leave the depths;
Neither should weapons of state ever be aired.

37.

Tao never does anything,
And everything gets done.

If a ruler can keep to it,
The ten thousand things
Will change of themselves.

Changed, things may stir desire.
Quiet them with the nameless simple,
Which alone brings no-desire.
No desire: then there is peace,
And beneath heaven
Will settle down of itself.

38.

High virtue is not virtuous;
Therefore it has virtue.
Low virtue is always virtuous;
Therefore it has no virtue.
High virtue does nothing
And has no ulterior ends.
Low virtue does something,
Also has ulterior ends.

High humanity has ulterior ends,
But it does something.
High morality does something,
Also has ulterior ends.
High ceremony does something,
And when it gets no response
It rolls up its sleeve and takes to force.

When Tao is lost, there is virtue.
When virtue is lost, there is humanity.
When humanity is lost, there is morality.
When morality is lost, there is ceremony.
Now ceremony is the shell of
Loyalty and trust
And the beginning of befuddlement.
As to foreknowledge,
It is a blossomy path
And the beginning of folly.

Therefore,
The fulfilled man holds to
The solid rather than the shell,
The fruit rather than the blossom.
He avoids the outward, accepts the inward.

39.

From of old,
There are those who reached oneness:
Heaven reached oneness and became clear;
Earth reached oneness and became tranquil;
Spirits reached oneness and became mystic;
Valleys reached oneness and became full;
The ten thousand things reached oneness
And became potent;
Barons and kings reached oneness
And became sovereign.
Did they not all become so
Through oneness?

If heaven were not clear,
It probably would crack.
If earth were not tranquil,
It probably would quake.
If spirits were not mystic,
They probably would desist.
If the valleys were not full,
They probably would die out.
If ten thousand things were not potent,
They probably would die off.
If barons and kings were not sovereign,
They probably would fall.

For the great has its roots in the humble;
The high has its foundation upon the low.
Barons and kings call themselves
The orphaned, the lonely, the unworthy:
Do they not have roots in the humble?
Truly,
The parts of a cart are not the cart.
Do not shine like jade
Or sound like stone chimes.

40.

Returning is the motion of Tao;
Softness is the utility of Tao.
All things in heaven and earth
Are born of being;
Being is born of non-being.

41.

When a superior man hears about Tao,
He goes after it diligently.
When an average man hears about Tao,
He both gets it and loses it.
When an inferior man hears about Tao,
He laughs loudly at it.
If he did not laugh,
It would not be Tao.

There is an old saying:
The bright way looks dark;

The forward way looks backward;
The smooth way looks rough;
High virtue looks low;
Great whiteness looks defiled;
Broad virtue looks deficient;
Solid virtue looks illicit;
Simple virtue looks decayed.
Great space has no corners.
Great talent ripens late.
Great music is out of key.
The great symbol is out of shape.

Tao is without name and hidden.
Hence Tao helps and completes.

42.

Tao bore one, one bore two, two bore three;
Three bore the ten thousand things.
The ten thousand things
Carry yin and embrace yang,
Whose blending breaths make them harmonize.

Men hate to be
Orphaned, lowly, unworthy,
Yet barons and kings
Use these names as titles.
Indeed,
You may gain by losing,
And you may lose by gaining.

What others have taught, I also teach:
Men of violence perish by it.
Whoever said this is
Father of my teaching.

43.

The softest things beneath heaven
Overcome the hardest.
Nothingness alone penetrates no-space.
Hence I know the use
Of nothing-doing.

The lesson of nothing-speaking,
The use of nothing-doing:
Rare attainments beneath heaven!

44.

Name and self, which is dearer?
Self and wealth, which is nearer?
Gain and loss, which hurts the worst?
For:
Attachment comes at wasteful cost;
Hoarding leads to certain loss;
Knowing what is enough avoids disgrace;
Knowing when to stop secures from peril.
Only thus can you long last.

45.

What is most perfect seems imperfect,
But using it doesn't use it up.
What is most full seems empty,
But using it doesn't wear it down.

Great straightness seems crooked;
Great skill seems clumsy,

Great eloquence seems hesitant.
Movement conquers cold,
But stillness conquers heat.

Clearness and serenity
Are beneath-heaven's norm.

46.

When beneath-heaven has Tao,
Race horses are used to fertilize fields.
When beneath-heaven has no Tao,
War horses breed in the suburbs.

No calamity is greater
Than not knowing what is enough,
No fault worse than wanting too much.
Whoever knows what is enough has enough.

47.

Without going out of the door
You can know beneath-heaven.
Without looking out of the window
You can see heaven's way.
The farther you go,
The less you know.

Thus the sage
Knows without walking,
Sees without looking,
And does without doing.

48.

To get learning, add to it daily.
To get Tao, subtract daily.
Subtract and subtract
Until you achieve nothing-doing.
Do nothing-doing
And everything will get done.
To win beneath-heaven
Always avoid fussing.
If fussing is not avoided,
Beneath-heaven is not won.

49.

The sage has no fixed heart.
He finds his heart
In the hundred families' hearts.
He is good to the good;
He is good to the not-good.
For virtue is good.
He is faithful to the faithful;
He is also faithful to the unfaithful,
For virtue is faithful.

Living beneath heaven,
The sage deals shyly with beneath-heaven
And simplifies his heart.
The hundred families strain eyes and ears;
The sage acts the child to all of them.

50.

Going out is life;
Coming back is death.

The companions of death are thirteen.
The companions of life are thirteen.
For people moving toward death
There are also thirteen.
How is that?
Because they overreach life.

It is said that
He who preserves his life
Meets no tigers or wild buffaloes on the road,
Remains untouched by weapons in the wars.
In him, the wild buffalo
Finds no space for his horns,
The tiger no space for his claws,
The soldier no space for his blade.
How is this?
Because there is no space for death in him.

51.

Tao gives them life;
Virtue nurses them;
Reality shapes them;
Chance completes them.
Thus the ten thousand things
All worship Tao and esteem virtue.
No one commands them
To worship Tao and esteem virtue.
They do so of themselves.

For Tao gives them life.
Virtue nurses them, raises them,
Nurses them, shelters them,
Comforts them, feeds them,
And protects them.
Rear but don't own!
Work but don't claim!

Raise but don't butcher!
This is called inward virtue.

52.

Beneath-heaven has a beginning:
The mother of beneath-heaven.
Knowing the mother,
We may know the children.
Knowing the children,
We may keep to the mother.
Death of body? No risk!

Block the passages,
Shut the doors:
End of life? No fuss!
Open the passages,
Meddle with things:
End of life? No help!

See the small: that is insight.
Keep to weakness: that is strength.
Use the light: go back to insight,
Keeping away from calamity
And practicing the changeless.

53.

If I have a grain of wisdom,
I walk along the great Tao
And only fear to stray.
The great Tao is easy indeed,
But the people choose by-paths.
The court is very resplendent;

But very weedy are the fields
And the granaries very empty.

They wear gaudy clothes,
Carry sharp swords,
Exceed in eating and drinking,
Have more riches than they can use.
Call them robber-braggarts:
They are anti-Tao indeed!

54.

What is well planted won't be uprooted;
What is well grasped won't slip away.
Sons and grandsons will keep the sacrifices.

Practice virtue in yourself:
Virtue becomes real.
Practice it in the family:
It becomes overflowing.
Practice it in the village:
It becomes lasting.
Practice it in the country:
It becomes prolific.
Practice it beneath heaven:
It becomes universal.

Thus persons are to be looked at
As a person,
Families as a family,
Villages as a village,
Countries as a country,
Beneath-heaven as beneath-heaven.
How do I know about beneath-heaven?
Inward Light!

55.

One who is weighty in virtue
Resembles an infant child.
Poisonous insects don't sting him;
Wild beasts don't seize him;
Birds of prey don't strike him.
His bonds are soft,
His sinews tender,
Yet his grip is strong.
He does not know
The union of male and female,
Yet his virility is evident,
His vitality perfect.
He cries and howls all day,
But does not get hoarse.
Perfect harmony!

To know harmony
Is to know the changeless.
To know the changeless
Is to have insight.
It is ominous
To improve on life,
Violent to
Control breathing by the mind:
Things overgrown fall into decay.
This is not-Tao,
And what is not-Tao soon ends.

56.

He who knows does not speak;
He who speaks does not know.

Block the passages!
Shut the doors,
Blunt edges,
Untie tangles,
Harmonize lights,
Unite all dust.
Call this the original oneness.
It can't be had by courting,
Can't be had by shunning;
Can't be had by helping,
Can't be had by harming;
Can't be had by praising,
Can't be had by blaming:
For it is beneath-heaven's highest.

57.

Govern the country by regular rules;
Direct the army by cunning moves;
But win the world by avoiding fuss.
How do I know that this is so?
Inward Light!

Beneath heaven
The more rules and prohibitions there are,
The poorer the people become.
The sharper the weapons are,
The greater the country's confusion.
The cleverer the people become,
The more cunning acts take place.
The more laws and orders there are,
The more thieves and robbers appear.

Therefore the sage says:
I do nothing,
And the people of themselves reform.

I love stillness,
And the people of themselves go straight.
I don't fuss,
And the people of themselves get rich.
I don't want,
And the people of themselves grow simple.

58.

When the law is dumb dumb,
The people are simple simple.
When the law is smart smart,
The people are broke broke.

Good fortune rests on bad fortune.
Bad fortune hides in good fortune.
Who knows the end of this?
It does not stop:
The normal turns into the odd;
The good turns into the weird.
Long have the people been in a stew!

Therefore the sage
Squares, but doesn't cut;
Exacts, but doesn't hurt;
Shapes, but doesn't strain;
Brightens, but doesn't dazzle.

59.

In ruling people and serving heaven,
It is best to be sparing.
To be sparing is to yield quickly.
To yield quickly is to double-store virtue.

If virtue is double-stored,
Nothing can't be overcome.
When nothing can't be overcome,
No one knows his limits.
When no one knows his limits,
That one can take on the country.
When that one takes on
The mother of the country,
He can last and endure.

Call this having deep roots
And a strong stem:
Living, lasting,
And seeing into Tao.

60.

Rule a big country
As you would cook a small fish.

When beneath-heaven is ruled with Tao,
Demons don't go spiriting.
Not only do the demons not spirit,
But the spirits don't harm people.
Not only do the spirits do no harm,
But the sage also does no harm.
Since both do no harm,
Virtue is restored intact.

61.

A great country is one that downward flows
To be a confluence of all beneath heaven
And beneath-heaven's female.

For the feminine overcomes the masculine
By quietude and lowliness.

Hence,
By lowering itself before a small country,
A great country wins over a small country.
By lowering itself before a large country,
A small country wins over a large country.
The one wins by lowering itself,
The other by keeping itself lowered.
Great countries wish nothing more
Than to shelter people;
Small countries wish nothing more
Than to have their people sheltered.
Since each gets its wish,
The great country ought to make itself lower.

62.

Tao is the refuge of the ten thousand things:
The treasure of the good man,
The backstop of the not-good man.
Fine words can be sold.
Noble deeds gain respect.
Even not-good people
Are not rejected.

When an emperor is enthroned
Or the three ministers installed,
Disks of jade and teams of horses
Are not as gifts the equal
Of sitting still and offering Tao.

Why did the ancients prize the Tao?
Because if it is sought, it is found;
Because the guilty are forgiven.
That is why it is beneath-heaven's treasure.

63.

Do nothing-doing;
Manage nothing-managing;
Taste nothing-tasting.
Exalt the low;
Multiply the few;
Repay hatred with virtue.

Tackle the difficult when it is easy.
Handle the big when it is small.
Difficult things beneath heaven
Are made up of easy things.
Big things beneath heaven
Are made up of small things.
Thus the sage
Never deals with the great,
But accomplishes greatness.

Light promises indeed lack trust.
Much easiness leads to much difficulty.
Thus the sage
Holds everything difficult,
But meets no difficulty in the end.

64.

What is at rest is easy to hold.
What hasn't happened is easy to forestall.
What is brittle is easy to break.
What is minute is easy to scatter.
Deal with a thing before it exists;
Handle disorder before it takes place.

A tree of a full span's girth
Springs from a tiny sprout.

A nine-story tower
Rises from a clod of earth.
A journey of a thousand miles
Starts from where your feet are.

Whoever acts spoils;
Whoever grasps loses;
The sage does nothing;
Therefore he spoils nothing.
He grasps nothing;
Therefore he loses nothing.

People often spoil things
At the point of success.
Take it easy
At the finish as well as the start;
Then nothing will be spoiled.

Therefore the sage
Desires to be desireless,
Does not prize rare goods,
Learns to unlearn his learning,
Returns the people to what they have lost,
Helps all things find their nature,
But dares not do.

65.

The ancients well versed in Tao
Did not enlighten the people
But kept them simple-minded.

Why are the people hard to govern?
Because they are too clever.
Clever government is a curse,
Non-clever government a blessing.

To know these two things
Is to follow the ancient pattern,
And to know the ancient pattern
Is original virtue.

Original virtue is far-reaching and deep.
It leads all things to return
Back to the great harmony.

66.

Rivers and seas
Become kings of the hundred valleys
Because they lie lower.
That is why they become kings.

Hence the sage,
Wishing to be higher than the people,
Keeps his speech lower;
Wishing to lead the people,
Puts himself behind them.

For the sage
Stays above the people,
But they don't feel weight;
Stays in front,
But they don't feel hurt.

Thus, beneath-heaven
Gladly upholds him
And does not weary of him.

Because he does not compete,
Nobody beneath heaven
Can compete with him.

67.

All beneath heaven say
My great Tao seems unlikely.
But it is great
Because it seems unlikely.
Were it not unlikely,
Long indeed would it have been petty.

I have three treasures,
Held close and guarded.
The first is love.
The second is simplicity.
The third is not-daring
To be first beneath heaven.
Whoever is loving can be brave;
Whoever is simple can be generous;
Whoever is not-daring
To be first beneath heaven
Can be a vessel of excellence.
But to be brave without being loving,
Generous without being simple,
Foremost without being hindmost,
This is to perish!

For:
Love cannot fight without winning,
Cannot defend without strengthening.
When heaven helps
It protects by loving.

68.

A good soldier is not violent;
A good fighter has no wrath.
The best way to win over an enemy

Is not to compete with him.
The best way to use a man
Is to work under him.
Call this not-competing in virtue.
Call this using human strengths.
Call this mating with heaven as of old!

69.

The strategists have a saying:
I dare not be a host,
But rather a guest;
Dare not advance an inch,
But rather retreat a foot.
This is called
Marching by not marching,
Capturing by not baring arms,
Charging by not attacking,
Holding by not bearing arms.

There is no evil heavier
Than to make light of an enemy.
To make light of an enemy
Is to lose what we value.
Thus when armies clash,
The one that grieves wins.

70.

My words are very easy to know,
Very easy to follow;
But beneath-heaven can't know them,
Can't follow them.

My deeds have an ancestor;
My deeds have a lord.
People don't know him,
So they don't know me.
The fewer who know me,
The more honored I am.

The sage wears coarse clothing,
Inside himself hides jade.

71.

To know and to be unknowing is best;
Not to know and to be knowing is sickness.
Only by being sick of our sickness
Are we not sick.

The sage is not sick.
He is sick of his sickness
And therefore not sick.

72.

When people don't fear force,
Greater force then comes upon them.
Don't meddle with their homes
Or weary them at their work.
Only when they are not wearied
Will they not weary you.

Therefore,
The sage knows himself,
But makes no show of himself.
Loves himself,
But does not exalt himself.

He rejects the outward,
Accepts the inward.

73.

The brave in daring die;
The brave in not-daring live.
Of these two,
One helps, the other hurts.
Heaven may hate,
But who knows why?
This question stumps the sage.

It is the Tao of heaven
To conquer without competing,
To answer without speaking,
To attract without summoning,
To plan without hastening.
Vast is heaven's net
And wide-meshed,
Yet nothing slips through.

74.

When people don't mind death,
Why threaten them with death?
If, afraid of death,
They were still unruly,
Who would dare to seize and kill them?

The great executioner
Kills those who kill.
To take his place is like
Handling the hatchet
For a master carpenter.
Whoever handles the hatchet

For a master carpenter
Usually get his hands cut.

75.

When people are starving,
Their rulers are taxing them heavily.
That is why they are starving.
When people are hard to govern,
Their rulers are something-doing.
That is why they are hard to govern.
When people make light of death,
Their rulers make much of life.
That is why they make light of death.

But not interfering with life
Is worthier than overreaching life.

76.

A man lives soft and weak,
Dies hard and stiff.
The grass, the trees,
The ten thousand things
Live soft and supple,
Die brittle and dry.

Hence
The hard and stiff
Are followers of death;
The soft and weak
Are followers of life.
For when armies are stiff,
They will lose;
When trees are stiff,

They will fall.
The stiff and mighty
Will be cast down;
The soft and weak
Will be lifted up.

77.

Heaven's Tao is like a stretched bow:
The top goes down
And the bottom goes up.
What has much is shortened;
What has little is increased.

Heaven's Tao takes from those with much
And gives to those with little.
Man's way is not so:
It takes from those with little
And gives to those with much.

Who uses muchness
To serve beneath-heaven?
Only he who has Tao!
Therefore the sage
Does but does not claim,
Completes but takes no credit.
He does not want his merit seen.

78.

Nothing beneath heaven
Is softer and weaker than water.
Nothing is better
To attack the hard and strong,

And nothing can take its place.
The weak overcome the strong;
The soft overcome the hard.

There is no one beneath heaven
Who doesn't know this,
And no one who practices it.

Therefore the sage says:
To bear the dirt of the country
Is to be master of the grain-shrines.
To bear the sins of the country
Is to be the lord of beneath-heaven.
Indeed, straight words seem crooked!

79.

When great ill-will is reconciled,
And there remains ill-will,
How shall it be made good?

By the sage holding the left-hand tally
And laying no guilt on others.
If you have virtue, you keep to the tally;
If you don't have virtue, you pyramid claims.
The Tao of heaven plays no favorites,
But it always succors the good.

80.

Oh for a small country with few people!
There may be contrivances
Of ten-fold or hundred-fold productivity,
But the people don't use them.

Let the people mind death
And not move away.
Though there are boats and carriages,
There is no occasion to ride them.
Though there are weapons and arms,
There is no occasion to show them.
Let the people again knot cords.
Let them enjoy their food,
Take pleasure in their houses,
And delight in their customs.

Another country may be so near
That each hears the noise
Of the other's cocks and dogs,
But until the end of their days,
The two people never mingle.

81.

True words are not nice;
Nice words are not true.
A good man does not argue;
An arguer is not good.
The wise are not learned;
The learned are not wise.

The sage does not hoard.
The more he does for others,
The more he has himself.
The more he gives,
The more he gets.

The Way of Heaven is
To benefit but not to harm.
The Way of the sage is
To work but not compete.

Acknowledgments

In the commentary, quotations from the Bible are from the Moffatt translation unless otherwise noted: *A New Translation of the Bible*, by James Moffatt, New York, Harper and Brothers, 1954. Appreciation is expressed to Harper and Row for permission to make use of the quotations. The initials KJV indicate the King James Version.

Identified in the commentary are the manuscript sources from which quotations by George Fox, Isaac Penington, John Woolman, and other early Quakers are taken. Punctuation and spelling have been modernized.

Quotations in the commentary from Hasidic stories and sayings and from the writings of Martin Buber are taken from books whose titles are abbreviated as follows: Tales: quoted with the permission of Schocken Books, Inc., from *Tales of the Hasidim: Early Masters*, by Martin Buber, Copyright © 1947 by Schocken Books, Inc.; Copyright renewed 1975 by Schocken Books, Inc. Hasidism: *Hasidism*, by Martin Buber, New York, Philosophical Library, 1948. The Way of Man: *The Way of Man, according to the Teachings of Hasidism*, by Martin Buber, Pendle Hill Pamphlets No. 106, by permission of Routledge and Kegan Paul, London, 1950. Two Types: *Two Types of Faith*, by Martin Buber, New York, The Macmillan Company, New York, 1951. Between: *Between Man and Man*, by Martin Buber, the Macmillan Company, New York, 1949. Appreciation for permission to make use of the quotations is expressed to the respective publishers. The quotation from Martin Buber on page 24 is from a

1928 address, "China and Us," included in *Pointing the Way: Collected Essays*, by Martin Buber, Harper and Brothers, 1957, pp. 124-125. Appreciation is expressed to Harper and Row for permission to use the quotation.

Appendix for Scholars
This for *That*

The aim of conventional translation is to make the original understandable, to set down ideas and concepts in one language that correspond to those of another. But what if the original is not conventional, if it is not understandable in the outward terms of concept and idea, if, in sum, the manner of the original is without a counterpart in the languages then and now current—particularly if the original deals with that which is almost beyond the limits of the verbally communicable? Translation of the Tao Teh Ching is further complicated by the necessity of reproducing in words based on sound the meaning of characters based on sight, but the problem of communicability is much deeper. How in any language shall anything be conveyed that taxes logical comprehension? Conveying the way, the manner, the inward sense of Lao Tzŭ is perhaps more significant than grasping the words he wrote.

Comparable difficulty exists with prophetic scriptures in general, certainly with the writings of early date selected for commentary in the present series of books. Hence the text of Lao Tzŭ's book of Tao has been placed first in this series and has been translated in full. Its textual problems are typical, and its length is sufficiently brief to permit presentation of one whole text without editing the problems away. Scripture is necessarily that which is revised; so important is it to its early generations of copyists that it is subject to reworking and to updating.

Comparison is possible with prophetic writings of relatively recent date. The very large output of Mahatma Gandhi on social and spiritual reality has been judged political in character. And the books and pamphlets of the seventeenth-century Quakers have become objects of a scholarly examination, which in turn has led to then-and-now misunderstanding. Later experts have applied an order of approach different from that of the early writers. Contemporary scholars studying the writings of founder George Fox often emphasize his outward language at the expense of his inward experience, and discuss his work in terms of system and belief. These are tools of current research in religion, but they are foreign to Fox's experiential sense of the power and presence of Truth. As a consequence, Fox is portrayed as a man with a set of formulated ideas and beliefs instead of a series of inward experiences. His words mean something to contemporary critics that they did not mean to him and the early Friends. The problems of *this* and *that*—inwardness and outwardness—thus join those of *then* and *now*.

To discern what Fox experienced, it may be necessary to sense it first in oneself. Similarly, it may be necessary to sense Tao in oneself in order to sense it in Lao Tzŭ. This sense, fortunately, can exist unconsciously as well as consciously, and it is present in degree in many commentaries and translations. Of the latter there are dozens in Western languages, of the former hundreds in Chinese.

Try *not* to make sense

These works are characterized by varying degrees of *this* and *that*. Of the two dissimilar ways of making sense of the Tao Teh Ching, one way is to decide what the original characters mean apart from the text, so that the text may be clarified and read intelligibly, a way that typically uses concepts and abstractions. Another way is to stick to the text and linger over it until its sense emerges, a way that emphasizes insight. The first way is to grasp the Tao Teh Ching; the second is to be hit by it.

For the book is not a reasoned, connected exposition, but rather a series of observations which, if read and reread sufficiently, lead to an inward experience of Truth and a way of social existence based on it. The Tao Teh Ching is not written in terms of logical connections but in terms of flashes of insight. It is not concerned with the rectification of terms by which Confucius set store, but with overwhelming spiritual vistas and floods of intense light not unlike those of Isaiah. The reader should not comprehend the book but be taken aback by it.

But if a translation of Lao Tzŭ aims at insight, it must begin with textual fact, for which solid research is prerequisite. Prophetic scriptures have indeed been altered repeatedly during the course of time (usually because succeeding generations try to contemporize them), but to convey effectively an inward message, they must be kept as close as possible to the inward hand that was originally upon them. One way of sticking to the original is an internal way: examining difficult words and passages in terms of the book in which they appear. Another way is external: examining them in terms of the language and ideas of other books thought to have been written contemporaneously with the book under translation.

Internal vs. external evidence

This latter approach has complicated translations of the Tao Teh Ching, for it has involved, in some cases, refurbishing the book in terms of the mental and emotional furniture of differing eras of Chinese history. Mr. Arthur Waley, famous scholar and translator, was persuaded, for example, that the Tao Teh Ching was written about 240 B.C., a date considerably later than the sixth century B.C., in which the book is traditionally located. While dating ancient texts is an interesting and innocent undertaking, innocence can disappear whenever dates are used to determine what the text means. For Mr. Waley and for scholars, Chinese and foreign, who follow his methods, dating the Tao Teh Ching can involve a large construct of external influences, on the basis of which its internal meaning is recast and rediscovered.

It is supposed, for instance, that the book's language and style can indicate its date, that date can define its meaning, and that date and meaning can locate the book in a supposed progression of ideas; and thus render clear whatever is not clear. "I see no way," writes Mr. Waley, "of making the text intelligible without showing how the ideas which it embodies came into existence." (Arthur Waley, *A Study of the Tao Te Ching and its Place in Chinese Thought,* London, Allen & Unwin, 1934, p.14.)

Dr. Hu Shih has noted the essential illogicality of such suppositions in his remarkable essay, "A Criticism of Some Recent Methods Used in Dating Lao Tzǔ," *The Harvard Journal of Asiatic Studies*, 2 (January): 1937, pp. 373-397. From ancient China there has come not a few but a whole series of difficult-to-date books, and Dr. Hu notes that they cannot be used to locate one another. Dr. Hu, a man of marked courtesy, calls fellow Chinese scholars to account for such procedures. The present translator seeks here to emulate his courtesy by questioning a fellow foreigner for using date to determine meaning.

Scripture vs. scholarship

Mr. Waley divides translations of Lao Tzǔ into the scriptural and historical (his term for the scholarly-scientific) and, while not condemning all scriptural translations (nor those he calls literary), insists that they are worthless for purposes of determining what the Tao Teh Ching originally meant. But let not his method be quickly dismissed. The method is common: as common, for instance, in commenting on ancient Hebrew texts as in commenting on those of ancient China. It is the method of the so-called higher criticism, and of the philology first developed in eighteenth century China, in that country's closest approach to the methodology of science. The present translation is based on the conviction that there is not a dichotomy between the scholarly and the scriptural (or literary), and that one type of approach can buttress the other. However a translation is constructed, it must obviously be based on the closest possible exactness of text. Similarly, it should reveal the *manner* of the text, not only the outward meaning of it. In most thoughtful translations of Lao Tzŭ, however, manner is taken little into account.

"Not not-know"

The primary issue of scholarly translations is a concern for the many linguistic factors that bear on exactness. Such translations are necessarily disquisitional; in the particular case of the Tao Teh Ching they fall out of tune with the elliptical and emphatic manner which is an essential part of the text. That manner, indeed, has led some translators to verbose explanation absent in the original. Literary translators need not, to be sure, fall back on discursiveness, but the search for precise meaning has enslaved them also. They too can suffer from verbosity. (Were they free of it, there would be no need for the present translation.) Wholeness is a great desideratum of the Tao Teh Ching; a translation of it should be able to proceed from exactitude of text to verbal impact and briskness of style. Chapter 5 uses only eight characters to say, "Many words exhaust sense. Keep to the empty center." Using nineteen words, Mr. Waley translates the passage thus: "Whereas the force of words is soon spent. Far better it is to keep what is in the heart." Even Dr. Wu is not succinct, requiring thirteen words: "No amount of words can fathom it. Better look for it within you."

The present translation aims to take a stylistic step forward in what may be called the literary-scholarly tradition of Dr. Wu and Dr. Lin in rendering Chinese texts. Why should this tradition be here followed? Why, when there are not a few excellent works in the scholarly-literary tradition? There are, to note two examples, careful and penetrating translations with accompanying commentary by Professor Wing-stit Chan and by Professor Robert G. Henricks, the first based on the Wang Pi text of the second century A.D. and the second on the new Mawangtui texts of the second century B.C. In 1973 the latter were found entombed in the village of Mawangtui in the province of Honan. Much earlier than the Wang Pi, they do not involve

239

basic changes in the message of the Tao Teh Ching, but they contain new words, sentences, and grammatical constructions.

The reader is referred to *Lao-Tzŭ, Te-Tao Ching, a New Translation Based on the Recently Discovered Ma-wang-tui Texts, Translated with an Introduction and Commentary,* by Robert G. Henricks, Ballantine Books, New York, 1989. For an excellent scholarly rendition of the Wang Pi text now in print, the reader is referred to Professor Chan's *The Way of Lao Tzŭ, a Translation and Study of the Tao Te Ching,* New York, Bobbs-Merrill, 1963, which appeared also in his compendium of translation and comment: *A Source Book of Chinese Philosophy,* Princeton, Princeton University Press, 1963, pp. 136-176.

Excellent as these books are, they suffer the problem of translations that aim for verbal definition and logical understanding, based on a large linguistic surround of varied definitions, alternate readings, possible variations, sundry etymological considerations, various historical influences, and comments of every description: in short, from the huge collection of external data and analysis that must be kept continually in the scholarly mind when studying or rendering the Tao Teh Ching. With so much in mind, there is necessarily little room for considerations of impact and style.

Newer vehicle or older vehicle

This translation opts for the literary-scholarly tradition. In opting for it, it opts also for the traditional Wang Pi text, now seemingly outdated but more exactly predated by the Mawangtui finds. This latter option may help explain the former. It is the argument of this writer that there was not a single line of copying and commenting by which the Tao Teh Ching was transmitted during the many centuries before the introduction of printing gave it permanence in the eighth century A.D. There may have been multiple lines of transmission, of which the Wang Pi and Mawangtui texts are illustrative but not exclusive.

Other lines may well have existed; still others, entombed with their creators (like the Mawangtui texts) may, encouragingly, await future discovery.

Not at any time since its appearance (whenever that may have been) was the Tao Teh Ching a work easy to take hold of in any ordinary grip. It undermines ordinary sense, tweaks the nose of propriety, and rails against knowledge of any conventional pattern. It is not so perplexing to persons already improper, unconventional, and lacking in sense, but it is to others. Yet to many of these others it is as intriguing and inviting as it is perplexing and paradoxical. So it must have been to many of the Confucian scholars, even though, early and late, they were upholders of outward order, careful study, and duty of an almost Miltonian severity. In them enough remained of the old Taoist tradition (probably much older than the Tao Teh Ching) for them to turn to it, not only for problems of governing, but for personal counsel, escape from court etiquette, inward encouragement, or elevation of mood.

That they did so later on in the documented days when scholars became China's landscape painters argues that they must have begun to do so earlier. They turned, perhaps with equal parts of fascination and surreptition, to the peculiar words of Tao to help understand the world and the emotion from which came part of their sense for the nature around them and later for their distinctive manner of painting it. But the texts at hand suggest that they had trouble taking in the words they were turning to.

When confronted with words that elude logical understanding but still compel attention, it is possible to gain some understanding by rewriting whatever text is at hand into a personalized document, adding and changing words, revising grammar, and creating punctuation marks with the worthy purpose of making clear what seems to be unclear. (The Taoist way, of course, would not be making anything clear but letting it become so of itself.) It is known that by early Han times there were dozens of commentaries on the Tao Teh Ching, and it seems likely that many of them were the personal copies of intrigued but baffled Confucianists. The change of a familiar for an unfamiliar character, the insertion of verbal direction posts, the extended use of particles to provide helpful punctuation, the omission of confusing phrases, and the addition of clarifying ones: these devices could lead to personalized texts and commentaries intended for private use. The Wang Pi text may have been just such a personalized work or the descendant of another such; so may the Mawangtui texts; so may texts yet to be discovered. So also are sundry transliterations of early English texts, which have had to be altered for twentieth century ears.

The ubiquity of personal texts

It is the conviction of this translator, as indicated above, that the Tao Teh Ching was written not to produce outward comprehension but to induce a form of inward shock. The book is staccato, not legato. Much use of particles, for instance, suggests an attempt to slow up the book and quiet it down. This suggestion, however, lends itself to literary and not scholarly verification. So, alack, do other suggestions pertinent to a multiple transmission thesis. But the use of different words in the two versions may indeed result not from linguistic complexity but from the simple explanatory use of familiar terms. The Mawangtui text seems at times to tend even toward the conventional. In Chapter 20, for example, the standard text reads, "What men fear must I fear?" while the Mawangtui text says, "The one who is feared by others, / Must because of this fear other men." And in Chapter 26, the two lines, "Though there are arresting sights, / He [the sage] does not stir but sits" becomes the following: "When he is safely inside a walled-in hostel and residing at ease— only then does he transcend all concern."

In most chapters, lines present in the Mawangtui texts are present in the standard text, but in some cases standard lines are not in the Mawangtui chapters, as for instance the famous do-nothing paradox at the end of Chapter 3: "By doing nothing, everything gets done." Nor does it appear in Chapter 48. A sound feeling for the Tao Teh Ching (evident in the Henricks translation) makes little of these differences, but persons trying to understand Lao Tzŭ in the early Han dynasty may well have been thrown by his paradoxes, as are some scholars today. Paradox, like satire, baffles conventional people. While there can be no final proof that the new texts are personal texts (the observations above are illustrative and not definitive), there is strong temptation to think them so.

Almost an eon and a half stretches between the traditional date of the Tao Teh Ching and the first copies of the printed version. It is customary to ascribe textual differences and irregularities during this interval to copyist mistakes, but many of the differences may result from simple perpetuation of personal texts. The differences seem to be the consequence not of error but of an effort to understand: a consideration that may help explain why various versions of the same text often depart so little in meaning one from the other. A sense of the sanctity of the written word has been at work.

In sum, it seems likely to this writer that different personal manuscripts led to different lines of transmission, of which two are now extant and of which there is hope of finding more. In such circumstances, one line of transmission is not by itself more valuable than another, and dates of appearance are not definitive as regards closeness of each manuscript to the original. It would seem that the Wang Pi version is not simply a later version in a single line of development, and not more subject to departure from the original manuscript, whatever that may have been, than the Mawangtui manuscripts. These, like the Wang Pi version, may have antecedents still unknown. But the writer's own acquaintance with the Tao Teh Ching has long been in terms of the Wang Pi text, and he does not now propose to change his tune.

In the words of Chuang Tzŭ, it is impossible to play two tunes at once. The components of the variant texts possess

243

a common message but not a common genealogy: they may have developed along parallel non-meeting lines. The nature of each may not only have been personal but also secret; the Tao Teh Ching was often banned. It seems wise not to treat any one line of text as definitive, but rather to pursue the separate lines. In these circumstances, earlier texts do not invalidate later ones.

Brevity and loquacity

Dr. John Wu says that people who lack a sense of *this*, the inward experience of reality, have trouble taking in the Tao Teh Ching, and that people who have such experience can unwittingly echo the book. He remarks in a footnote to Chapter 52: "Perhaps it takes a simple man to understand Lao Tzŭ." His translation was recommended by Dr. Hu Shih to the present translator in 1942. Dr. Wu never forgets that the Tao Teh Ching is not *that* but *this*, but, as noted earlier, his translation too tends toward discursiveness. The present translator has sought to convey the startling impact of the Tao Teh Ching on himself when he first began to be able to penetrate the original text. He remains convinced that the manner of the book is as important as its content and thus addresses his commentary and translation first of all to the general reader, translating for manner as much as for meaning. The incomprehensible is left incomprehensible.

To the specialized reader apologies should be extended for referring to Lao Tzŭ as if he were a person and not a scholarly designation, and for going so far into the realm of the legendary as to repeat Ssŭ-ma Ch'ien's story of the withdrawal to the barbarians. But handed-down legend suggests much that cannot otherwise be seen. It reveals the impact of an ancient teaching, older than the Tao Teh Ching itself, upon thousands of years of Chinese life and, through the book itself, reveals the pertinence of that teaching everywhere else.

Lao Tzŭ: TAO
Index

Alphabetized Index of Titles in Commentary
(Chapter numbers in parentheses)

Alphabetized Index of First Lines in Text
(Chapter numbers in parentheses)

Herrymon Maurer wrote eight published books on East Asia, prophetic religion, and the large corporation. During the Sino-Japanese War he taught English in West China and in 1942 became an editor of FORTUNE magazine. Thereafter, he wrote eight additional books on prophetic religion, the publication of which is now being undertaken. He was active since 1939 in the Religious Society of Friends (Quakers), of which he was a Recorded Minister of Princeton Monthly Meeting. He served as a trustee for sundry charitable organizations. His books were published in Britain, France, Japan, Argentina, Brazil, Canada, and the United States. His articles appeared in FORTUNE, Life, the Reader's Digest, the old Commentary, the New Leader, and other magazines. He died in 1998.

www.ingramcontent.com/pod-product-compliance
Lightning Source LLC
LaVergne TN
LVHW091214080426
835509LV00009B/992